More Praise for *VEGAN AL FRESCO*:

Summer is sure to sparkle a little brighter with this awesome cookbook as your dining. Whether you choose the backyard, nearby park, or cozy balcony as your on Carla Kelly to dish up a feast of melt-in-the-mouth recipes, as well as great tips gestions. *Vegan al Fresco* is a must have! —Zel Allen, author of *Vegan for the Holidays* *Nut Gourmet*, co-publisher of *Vegetarians in Paradise*

If you've ever been invited to a potluck, summertime barbecue, or other outdoorsy meal, and found yourself fretting over what deliciously creative vegan dish you could possibly bring along with you, you're in expert hands: Carla Kelly offers a bounty of brilliant recipes in *Vegan Al Fresco*, with useful tips and beautiful photography to boot. —Celine Steen, co-author of *Vegan Sandwiches Save the Day!* and *Whole Grain Vegan Baking*

Whether you are planning a family feast on the patio, or a romantic dinner on a blanket under the stars, *Vegan al Fresco* is packed with recipes that will fit the occasion. Cooking for a crowd, or your few closest friends, this book makes it easy and is a sure guide to successful entertaining. —Tamasin Noyes, author of *American Vegan Kitchen* and *Grills Gone Vegan*

Vegan picnic fare is so much more than PB&J sandwiches, chips, and fruit, and Carla Kelly's *Vegan al Fresco* proves that. From Samosa Spring Rolls and Cider-Battered Tofu to Pita Po' Boys and Brandied Tempeh Pate, Kelly takes the average picnic up quite a few notches. Plus, she includes ideas for non-food-related picnic activities (badminton, anyone?) and tips for bringing along your four-legged friends. —Bianca Phillips, author of *Cookin' Crunk: Eatin' Vegan in the Dirty South*

Full of fresh, fun ideas and perfected classics, Carla has done it again with *Vegan al Fresco*. Recipes focus on playing up the delicious flavors that nature has to offer, maximizing flavor while minimizing the work. Best of all, the wide variety allows for mix-and-matching, making this book full of combinations that will make you the star at any gathering you go to, using readily available ingredients. —Kris Peters Holechek, author of *100 Best Vegan Baking Recipes*

Whether you're looking to host a summer get-together, or wondering what to bring to a non-vegan cookout, Carla offers recipes for traditional fare with a unique twist. Packed with useful information and lovely photos, *Vegan al Fresco* will become a go-to cookbook for entertaining, barbecues, and picnics. —Kelly Peloza, author of *Cheers to Vegan Sweets* and *The Vegan Cookie Connoisseur*

Real food and easy-to-follow recipes that inspire creativity and health. —Vanessa Mills, owner of Chomp Vegan Eatery

Arsenal Pulp Press Vancouver

VEGAN al fresco

happy & healthy recipes for picnics, barbecues & outdoor dining

CARLA KELLY

VEGAN AL FRESCO
Copyright © 2014 by Carla Kelly

ARSENAL PULP PRESS
Suite 202–211 East Georgia St.
Vancouver, BC V6A 1Z6
Canada
arsenalpulp.com

The publisher gratefully acknowledges the support of the Government of Canada (through the Canada Book Fund) and the Government of British Columbia (through the Book Publishing Tax Credit Program) for its publishing activities.

The author and publisher assert that the information contained in this book is true and complete to the best of their knowledge. All recommendations are made without the guarantee on the part of the author and publisher. The author and publisher disclaim any liability in connection with the use of this information. For more information, contact the publisher.

Note for our UK readers: measurements for non-liquids are for volume, not weight.

Design by Gerilee McBride
Interior photographs and food styling by
    Tracey Kusiewicz/Foodie Photography
Editing by Susan Safyan
Author photo by Ellaird Photography

Printed and bound in China

Library and Archives Canada Cataloguing in Publication:

Kelly, Carla, 1971–, author
    Vegan al fresco : happy & healthy recipes for picnics, barbecues & outdoor dining / Carla Kelly.

Includes index.
Issued in print and electronic formats.
ISBN 978-1-55152-532-7 (pbk.).—
ISBN 978-1-927032-24-4 (epub)

    1. Vegan cooking. 2. Outdoor cooking.
3. Barbecuing. 4. Picnics. 5. Cookbooks. I. Title.

TX837.K45 2014   641.5'636   C2014-900265-3
                                 C2014-900266-1

For the next generation.
Trying to leave you a better world. (Hatchol).*

HFS
04/1999

MPK
02/2002

JJS
07/2002

RKK
12/2004

BLS
03/2012

*This is a made-up word that we use in my family—it means
"I love you the most."

Contents

Preface

Welcome to *Vegan al Fresco*! I believe food tastes best when it's shared with laughter and love—and with friends and family. The cookbooks I have written, including this one, are all about food that's tasty, full of flavor, and a little experimental, with easy-to-follow recipes to enjoy with others.

You'll find that I'm not hung up on low-fat, low-carb, or low-any-thing, really; I just try to use the best ingredients that nature provides (augmented here and there for convenience) to provide healthy, happy food that will enthral your taste buds. Originally from New Zealand, I'm a bit of a traveler, so my recipes have been influenced not only by the food I grew up with, but also by foods that I've tried and learned to love along the way.

After completing my second book (*Quick and Easy Vegan Slow Cooking*, 2012), I was more than ready to put the slow cooker back in the cupboard and get out the barbecue. The recipes in this book came from ideas I developed while doing lots of cooking and dining out-of-doors. And based on my research, I discovered that there is a need for this kind of a book; on any given online vegan food forum, you'll find threads along the lines of, "I've been invited to a cookout/barbecue/picnic. What should I make?" Vegans clearly need

a book that answers this question, and *Vegan al Fresco* is packed with bright, summery recipes to take with you to the great outdoors or to enjoy in the backyard at home. I've also attempted to answer some of the "What do I do with all this [insert summer produce name here]" questions (another common thread), which often arise as home gardens and farmers' markets fill with summer's bounty.

The recipes and ideas featured here make wonderful meals (from brunch to dinner and dessert) for patio or balcony dining, cookouts, barbecues, picnics, day-hiking trips, close-to-home camping, or even "glamping" (short for glamorous camping, i.e., with electricity and running water). For many of the recipes, you'll first need to have access to basic kitchen facilities—a refrigerator, a freezer, a grill or oven, and standard kitchen utensils and appliances.

In the Appendices, you'll find a list of theme menus for picnics and barbecues (such as "Passage to India" or "Wild Southwest," as well as 4th of July and Canada Day menus). There's also a list describing special vegan ingredients that are used throughout the recipes; many are available in conventional supermarkets and others from

specialty markets or health food stores. If you have food allergies or sensitivities to gluten, soy, or nuts, look for the symbols **g** **s** **n**.

While this book is almost completely summer-focused, using ingredients that are fresh in the warmer months, all of these recipes can be enjoyed indoors and in other seasons too. The recipes have been tested by my team of testers (from all over the world), so they're reliably foolproof. The result is a handy and inclusive vegan guide to the delights of al fresco dining. Enjoy!

Introduction: Where to Dine al Fresco?

Where will you host your outdoor dining extravaganza? I'm sure you have a great place in mind, whether it's your own backyard, a park down the street, or somewhere a little further afield. The advantage of choosing someplace close to home is that everything you need can be easily carried and set up (and you can always nip back home if the weather suddenly changes or you forget the ketchup!). When choosing a location slightly farther from home, consider the following:

- Does the location offer facilities for cooking, such as built-in barbecues, or can you take your own? Some parks will allow small tabletop grillers; others will allow you to use only their built-in barbecues, which need to be reserved.
- Are there seating areas with tables and benches? Do those need to be reserved along with the barbecue?
- How far away are the nearest washrooms? Sure, you can take antiseptic wipes for your hands (and you should), but facilities like this are important too.
- If you're planning to play games (see p. 13 for some great ideas) or

have energetic children with you, make sure there's space for running about or a play-park structure nearby.

- Are there trails for exploring, a creek to follow, or a beach on which to search for shells?
- Is the location animal-friendly? Is there an off-leash park nearby so that you can give your pet(s) a good run?
- Is there a shelter from possibly inclement weather—an undercover area or free-standing tent or some large umbrellas?

Remember to protect everyone from excess sun: "Slip, Slop, Slap" (slip on a shirt, slop on the sunscreen, slap on a hat), and drink lots of water if it's a hot day. There are many vegan brands of sunscreen available.

What to Bring Besides the Picnic Basket

The equipment you'll need for your picnic depends on the location, the style of event you're hosting, and how fancy you want to make it. Some of the following items will be essential and many will make your outdoor dining experience not only more pleasurable but safer.

- Blankets or mats
- Folding lawn chairs
- Folding table(s)
- Tablecloth(s)
- Tent, canopy, or large table/sun umbrella
- Matches and/or lighter
- Fuel (charcoal briquettes)
- Aluminum foil
- Squeeze bottle with cooking oil
- Tongs and spatulas for handling food
- Spray bottle with water for any flare-ups
- Serving platter(s) for hot foods
- Coolers and picnic baskets or soft-shell insulated packs and hikers' backpacks
- Cool packs, ice, and/or ice packs
- Re-usable, washable, airtight plastic containers
- Serving utensils
- Cutlery (washable metal or hard plastic)
- Serrated knife and cutting board
- Plates and glasses (unbreakable, washable acrylic)
- Napkins (preferably washable cloth)
- Dishcloths or antiseptic cleaning wipes
- Hand-sanitizing antiseptic gel or towelettes
- Bags, both large and small, for trash/litter and ziplock bags for items to be taken home
- Insect repellant and/or citronella candles
- Sunscreen and sun hats
- A fist-aid kit

Keep It Green

Follow these simple tips to respect the environment in which you're dining and make sure you can go back to the same spot, year after year. Go ahead—start a sustainable tradition!

• Check out the location before planning your event; take note of any environmentally sensitive areas such as new tree plantings, creek protection programs, and wildlife sanctuary areas that might be off-limits.
• Take care not to disturb flora and fauna.
• Respect the "Keep off the Grass" signs.
• As the old maxim says, "Take only photographs and leave only footprints."
• Try to leave the site in a cleaner condition than you found it; make "clean-up" the final activity of the day, encouraging all to take part.

You can take environmental awareness back to the sources of the food you're serving. Buy local produce from farmer's markets, organic if available and affordable. The shorter distance your food has traveled, the less pollution and waste it has created. Think seasonal, ripe, and fresh. Minimize the unrecyclable and non-reuseable plastics you purchase.

Something for Everyone

When menu planning, make sure there are enough options provided so that everyone will be able to have at least a taste of each dish. Ensure that specific tastes or dietary requirements are also catered for. You don't have to provide everything yourself, so coordinate and delegate—make it a potluck! For ideas on themed picnics and barbecues, see Appendix, p. 249. Recipes that contain soy, gluten, or nuts are marked with symbols, shown on p. 15.

When camping, the tools, equipment, and supplies you need will depend on whether you have a trailer or a tent and what kinds of facilities are available at your campsite. If you have a full-service site or trailer with running water, electricity, and access to a stove, you'll easily be able to make any of the recipes in this book. If not, then focus on food which suits the cooking facilities you have. If you have only a grill, items to barbecue (pp. 150–179) are great, but if you also have a small portable stove with a frying pan, then you can make dishes such as Aussie Falafel (p. 102) or Meat-y Ball Sandwiches (p. 106).

For campfires, anything that can be cooked on a stick is ideal, such as vegan hot dogs or bannock (flour mixed with baking powder and some water to make a rustic dough). You can also bake potatoes once the fire has burned down to embers (prick potato skins with a fork, wrap in foil, and place in hot embers for an hour or so, turning every now and then).

You can even make a yummy campfire dessert by slitting open a banana in its skin, inserting a piece of vegan chocolate, then wrapping in foil and baking in embers for 15 minutes until the chocolate is melted. (Take care eating this when hot, please!) Then, of course, there are s'mores (graham crackers, vegan chocolate, and vegan marshmallows) to make yourself a sticky but delicious treat.

Food Safety

You will want everyone to remember your picnic or outdoor meal for the wonderful food and company, not for the food-borne bacteria that laid them up for days! Follow these essential food-safety rules for a happy and healthy al fresco experience.

• Keep all foods chilled to 39°F (4°C) or below (refrigerator temperature) before cooking or serving—including during transportation and while in storage at the site.
• Ensure you have enough ice and/or cold packs to keep food chilled.
• Cooked protein-rich foods (this includes prepared products that you have purchased) should not be kept at room temperature for longer than 2 hours.

- Foods that are meant to be eaten cold need to be kept cold.
- Foods that are meant to be eaten hot need to be served very hot.
- Foods that have been preserved, such as pickles, relishes, and jams, are not "safe," but pose a much lower risk, if not kept chilled.
- Before packing it with food, clean the inside of your cooler with an antiseptic wipe, or wash it with hot soapy water. You don't want to put pristine food into a dirty cooler.
- Wash fruits and vegetables before packing to remove chemicals and soil-based pathogens, which are another cause of food-borne illness.
- Make sure you have used good food-handling practices at home (such as frequent hand-washing and effective cooling techniques) during the preparation of all food items.
- When preparing hot foods at home ahead of time, remember to allow time to cool them to room temperature before putting them into the refrigerator; refrigerating them too quickly can encourage the growth of illness-causing bacteria. Food should be cooled to below 50°F (10°C), within 2 hours of cooking.
- To cool food quickly, create as large a surface area as possible (think wide shallow tray rather than deep narrow one), and for a super speedy cool, create an ice (or cold water) bath for food containers.

- Prepare items in advance and chill in the refrigerator (or the freezer for any items which can be cooked from frozen such as commercially prepared veggie burgers) before packing. Don't expect the ice in the cooler to be able to chill warm items sufficiently—you're just asking for trouble.
- Use air-tight containers for all foods, so melting ice doesn't introduce water (and potentially bacteria).
- Use separate coolers for food and for drinks.
- Place last-to-be-used items (dessert, usually) at the bottom of the cooler, cover with a layer of ice or cool packs, then work upward, layering ice or cool packs in between courses, so that the uppermost layer is the first to be used or served.
- Pack the cooler until it is full, adding a layer of ice packs at the top if necessary. Keep the cooler firmly closed until mealtime to maintain the temperature inside. When traveling to the site, place your cooler in the coolest part of the vehicle (not necessarily the trunk). Once at the site, place the cooler in the shade.
- At the picnic or barbecue, follow safe food-handling procedures; ensure everyone who will be handling food washes their hands before doing so.

- Do not take home (other than to dispose of, in an animal-friendly/safe manner) any leftovers.
- After the picnic or barbecue, wash out the inside of the cooler with soap or an antiseptic solution. Completely dry the cooler before storing; the musty smell that sometimes wafts out of a rarely used cooler is due to bacterial growth.

Games & Activities

A quick game of tag or hide-and-seek while the spread is being prepared and cooked will get picnic appetites pumping. If the venue has trails, make use of them; enjoy a pre- or post-meal hike—you may discover some interesting things. If there is a safe beach, lake, river, creek, or swimming pool, bring your swimsuits along and have a splash to cool down before eating.

If there's room to pack it and room to use it once at the location, consider taking some sports equipment to your picnic site, such as:

- A badminton or volleyball net with either racquets or shuttlecocks and a ball. Some venues may have nets you can reserve or rent.
- A bat, a baseball, and a glove. (If there's no ball diamond, use natural objects or clothing as bases or simply play a game of catch.)

- A football for touch football (rather than the rougher tackle version, so everyone can join in). Mark the goal line using natural objects, clothes, or other items.
- A soccer ball for either an organized game or just a free-for-all kick-about.
- Items for catch games such as Frisbee.

Whatever activity you choose, make sure you play safe!

- Leave a large area between where you are playing and other groups of people.
- Make sure everyone is wearing proper shoes if doing lots of running around.
- Don't forget to reapply sunscreen on a regular basis, and take breaks to drink water and cool off.
- If there is a swimming facility, wait at least half an hour after eating before you swim.
- Oh, and if you'd like to take music? Play it softly so you don't disturb other people in the area.

Animals, Companion & Otherwise

If you plan to take your dog(s) with you, make sure you also take things for them to do—bring a ball or Frisbee (or even just a stick), so they can have fun as well. Don't forget to take a leash, chew toy (or other favorite toy), treats, and those little plastic bags so that when you walk them away from the eating area to do their business, you do the right thing. Ensure your furry friend has a spot in the shade to call their own and access to lots of clean water from the water bowl you brought. Double-check the environmental sensitivity of any area you'll be taking your animal pals to, and don't let them off-leash unless the area is specifically designated as such.

While your companion animals can add a lot of fun to an outdoor dining experience, wild animals just don't. The most important thing to remember when dining out-of-doors is not to feed wild animals, either on purpose or accidentally by leaving food scraps behind. Human food can make wild animals ill; it may also encourage them to become accustomed to eating human leftovers, which is not doing them (or people) any favors. Scavengers, such as squirrels, birds, raccoons, and yes, even coyotes and bears, may get used to finding discarded human food if left in areas such as campgrounds, picnic sites, or parks. For them, getting to eat your leftovers is a lot less work than finding their own food, and they may return to the site to seek out human food again. Ensure you take away any leftovers, or dispose of them in animal-safe rubbish bins.

Then there are the inevitable pesky picnic pests. First, check any area where you plan to picnic—before you set up—for wasp nests or ant hills, and move if you discover one. Cover any food left unattended to discourage flies and wasps, and put away leftovers immediately. A little diatomaceous earth (a natural clay that acts as an ant, cockroach, and slug repellant) may be sprinkled at the bottom of table legs to prevent pests from climbing up. *Caution*: Keep this away from food; it may be natural, but it is not safe to eat!

To stop biting bugs, such as mosquitoes, from becoming annoying, check out the numerous natural repellants available online or in health food stores. If you want to purchase a commercially made one, look for vegan brands such as Beat It!, Buzz Away, Jason Bug Off, or Moov, among others. I recommend avoiding anything that has DEET as an ingredient on the label; this compound can cause skin irritation and, apparently, a host of other health issues if not used carefully and correctly. Set up citronella candles as a perimeter around your picnic or barbecue; as they burn, they'll repel the insects. Search "repel insects naturally" online for plenty of alternatives, some of which you can make yourself.

Mix 1 tsp vanilla extract with 1 cup (250 mL) water in a spray bottle and spray as required to use for a pleasant smelling, insect-repelling solution.

If bees and wasps become a problem, place a sweet item, such as a very ripe, juicy piece of fruit or a bowl of juice, away from the main dining area, so the insects can partake of their share far away from you. If someone in your party is stung by a bee, the best thing to do—unless they have allergy issues—is to flick, not squeeze, the stinger out, and apply ice to minimize the swelling. *Note:* People with known allergies to bees and wasps shouldn't leave home without an epinephrine autoinjector.

Remember to take a first aid kit. (Do you keep a kit in your car? Bring it with you.) You never know when a knife may slip, someone will bump into a hot grill or fall down and skin a knee, so a basic supply of band-aids, antiseptic cream, and clean gauze to augment the ice you have in the cooler is a proactive and practical idea. Also ensure you have a fully charged cell phone with you, so you can call for help (as long as there is a signal) if anything more serious happens.

Allergen Symbols

Recipes that contain major allergens—gluten, soy, and nuts—are marked using the following symbols:

See also the Allergens List, p. 255.

I KNOW YOU'RE ITCHING TO GET *to the recipes so you can start to plan your next picnic or cookout, but first, let's start with five basic mixtures that are used over and over again in the recipes that follow.*

basic
recipes

Dry Chees-y Mix

Initially inspired many years ago by the recipe for "Dragonfly's Bulk Dry Uncheese Mix," which can be found on VegWeb.com, this is handy to keep in your refrigerator or freezer. It can be used as the base for sauces and dressings and adds a savory, cheesy flavor to recipes.

MAKES 2½ CUPS (625 ML)
Preparation time: *5 minutes*

½ cup (125 mL) raw cashews

½ cup (125 mL) quick-cooking rolled oats

¼ cup (60 mL) hemp seeds (see p. 251)

2 tbsp raw pine nuts

1 cup (250 mL) nutritional yeast (see p. 251)

¼ cup (60 mL) arrowroot powder (see p. 250)

1 tbsp garlic powder

1 tbsp onion powder

½ tsp salt

½ tsp ground dry mustard

¼ tsp ground cumin

¼ tsp ground turmeric

In a food processor, pulse together cashews, oats, hemp seeds, and pine nuts to form a smooth and lump-free powder. Stop to scrape sides of bowl as required. Add remaining ingredients and pulse to combine. Store in a sealed container in refrigerator or freezer for up to 2 months.

Pine nuts are the edible seeds of pine trees.

Chees-y Sauce
MAKES 1 CUP (250 ML)

In a small saucepan, combine ½ cup (125 mL) Chees-y Mix with ½ cup soy (or other) milk and ½ cup water. Heat on medium, stirring frequently for 8–10 minutes, until thickened. Taste and season with salt and pepper as desired.

Chees-y Salad Dressing
MAKES ¼ CUP (60 ML)

In a small bowl, combine ¼ cup (60 mL) vegan mayonnaise such as Tofonnaise (p. 110) with 1 tbsp Chees-y Mix and whisk to combine. Taste and season with salt and pepper as desired.

Faux Poultry Seasoning Mix

Sure, you can buy a commercial blend of poultry seasoning mix from the store, but this is super easy to whip up at home, and you can customize it to your taste. The mixture will store as long as regular dried herbs, about 6 months.

MAKES ¼ CUP (60 ML)
Preparation time: 5 minutes

4 tsp ground sage

2 tsp dried thyme

2 tsp dried crushed rosemary leaves

1 tsp dried oregano

1 tsp dried marjoram, or more oregano

1 tsp onion powder

1 tsp garlic powder

¼ tsp ground nutmeg

¼ tsp ground white pepper

¼ tsp celery salt or sea salt

1 bay leaf

In a small resealable container, mix together sage, thyme, rosemary, oregano, marjoram, onion powder, garlic powder, nutmeg, pepper, and celery salt. Add bay leaf, seal, and store until ready to use.

Wherever I've called for this to be used in the recipes that follow, you can substitute a commercial blend.

Stovetop Poached Garlic (opposite)

Cheater Sour Cream (p. 23)

Dry Chees-y Mix (p. 18)

Faux Poultry Seasoning Mix (p. 19)

Tandoori Spice Mix (p. 22)

Stovetop Poached Garlic & Garlic-Infused Oil

The component parts of this recipe can be used in a myriad of ways: use the oil in any recipe that needs a little mellow garlic flavor or drizzle it over a plated meal or salad; use the poached garlic wherever you would use roasted or raw garlic.

MAKES ½ CUP (125 ML) OIL & ABOUT 22 POACHED GARLIC CLOVES
Preparation time: 1½ hours

2 garlic heads, separated into cloves, base removed, peeled, about 22–24 cloves
½ cup (125 mL) canola, grapeseed, or other neutral-flavored oil

In a medium non-reactive saucepan on medium heat, combine garlic and oil, cover, and bring to a simmer. Reduce heat to lowest temperature and continue simmering, covered, for 45 minutes or until garlic is very soft (test by piercing with a fork).

Turn off heat and let saucepan sit on element for a further 30 minutes. Remove from element and let sit until cooled to room temperature.

Transfer to a glass jar and store in refrigerator. Will keep for up to 1 month.

Tandoori Spice Mix

This authentic-tasting spice mix is balanced and flavorful without being too spicy. Make a batch to keep in your cupboard and store at room temperature for up to 6 months.

MAKES ¼ CUP (60 ML)
Preparation time: 5 minutes

1½ tbsp ground cumin

2 tsp smoked paprika

1 tsp ground turmeric

1 tsp ground white pepper

1 tsp ground coriander

1 tsp ground cardamom

1 tsp ground ginger

½ tsp ground cloves

½ tsp ground cinnamon

¼ tsp chili flakes, or more to taste

In a small airtight container, mix all ingredients together.

Cheater Sour Cream

Although buying vegan sour cream is convenient, it's easy to make your own at home, and the bonus is that you know what all the ingredients are.

MAKES ¾ CUP (185 mL)
Preparation time: *10 minutes + 1½ hours chilling*

½ cup (125 mL) plain soy milk
2 tbsp full fat canned coconut milk
4 tsp lemon juice
2 tsp apple cider vinegar
1 tsp lime juice
¼ tsp salt
1 tbsp cornstarch
salt, ground black pepper, and lemon juice, to taste

In a small saucepan, stir together soy and coconut milks, lemon juice, vinegar, lime juice, and salt.

Add cornstarch and whisk until dissolved.

On medium heat, stirring frequently, heat mixture for 5 minutes, until just at a boil and thickened.

Remove from heat and immediately transfer to a small bowl. Let sit at room temperature for 30 minutes to cool. If a skin forms, stir it in with a fork.

Cover and chill for at least 1 hour to thicken. If too thick, whisk again and add water 1 tsp at a time until desired consistency.

Taste and season as desired.

JUST ABOUT EVERYTHING IN THIS *chapter can (and maybe should) be eaten with your fingers—no need for forks and knives! Create a perfect evening with friends on the balcony or patio as the sun goes down with a little bit of this served with a little bit of that and a glass of wine (or other beverage of choice). Pair, if you like, with some of the dips (p. 52–85) for a more substantial spread, or just keep things simple and offer one nibble to start before putting the main course on the grill and laying out the salads. If you like, you can complement some of the recipes in this chapter with store-bought treats such as olives, pickled vegetables, and fancy vegan cheese. When transporting finger foods to your picnic, use shallow containers that hold the items in one layer; they're easy to stack in a cooler and are also handy for serving.*

bites, nibbles & finger foods

Trail Mix

Trail mix is the perfect snack to nibble on as you hike to your picnic spot. I don't have a standard recipe; it changes from time to time depending on what I feel like and what I have in the house. I use nuts, seeds, and dried fruit as the base and add other ingredients as accents; see list below for some suggestions. I like to pack the mix in individual serving-sized ziplock plastic bags; if it spills, only a small amount is wasted. Each person can also add their favorites, to taste.

Nuts

Plain, roasted, flavored, or even caramelized, choose a single nut or in combination—almonds, pecans, walnuts, pistachios, Brazil nuts, hazelnuts, cashews, peanuts, soy nuts.

Dried fruits

Chop larger fruits into bite-sized pieces. Include raisins, golden raisins, cranberries, blueberries, apricots, apples, papaya, banana chips, pineapple, mango, cherries, crystallized ginger, freeze-dried strawberries, or large coconut shreds.

Seeds

Raw or toasted sunflower, pumpkin, hemp, or sesame.

Chocolate or carob

Use dark, vegan milk or vegan white chocolate (or a combination) chips or chunks, a chopped-up chocolate bar, or vegan chocolate candy. Choose carob, chocolate-covered peanuts, or raisins for variety.

And…

Whatever takes your fancy, be it vegan mini-marshmallows, store-bought or home-made granola or a vegan cereal of choice, cinnamon or other spices, peanut or Savory Sunflower Brittle (p. 28) in small pieces, vegan hard candy or toffee, or mini-crackers or pretzels.

Chili Roasted Chickpeas

These are tasty and spicy, good served hot or cold, and make a great outdoor party treat. They're also wonderful sprinkled over salads or mashed potatoes (try it!). I have been known to simply eat them with a spoon.

MAKES 2 CUPS (500 mL)
Preparation time: 5 minutes
Cooking time: 20 minutes

2 cups (500 mL) cooked chickpeas, or 1 19-oz (540-mL) can, drained, rinsed, and patted dry
2 garlic cloves, minced
1 jalapeño pepper, minced
1½ tbsp olive oil
½ tsp smoked paprika
½ tsp salt
¼ tsp chili flakes
¼ tsp Tandoori Spice Mix (p. 22) or curry powder
¼ tsp ancho chili powder (see p. 250)
⅛ tsp ground black pepper

Preheat oven to 425°F (220°C).

Toss all ingredients together on a large rimmed baking sheet, spreading in a single layer.

Bake for 10 minutes, turn, and bake for another 10 minutes, until chickpeas look dry and golden.

Savory Sunflower Brittle

I wanted to make an alternative to peanut or sesame brittle that would be neither too sweet nor too savory, but still resonate both tastes. Sweet and savory—this brittle hits the spot. When broken into little pieces, it's great as a hiking snack or tossed over salad and makes an attractive finish to sweet or savory dishes when left in larger pieces.

MAKES 2–4 SERVINGS

Preparation and cooking time:
15 minutes + 1½ hours firming

½ cup (125 mL) raw sunflower seeds
½ tsp dried crushed thyme
½ tsp dried crushed rosemary
¼ tsp salt
⅛ tsp ground black pepper
⅓ cup (80 mL) sugar

Line a large flat plate with parchment paper.

In a large frying pan on medium heat, toast sunflower seeds for about 7 minutes, until browned and aromatic. Stir in dried herbs, salt, and pepper and mix to coat.

Add 1 tbsp water. Stir in sugar and mix well. Allow sugar to melt. Stir to combine well and thoroughly coat seeds. Pour mix onto prepared plate and spread to a single layer.

Cool to room temperature for about 30 minutes, then refrigerate for 1 hour until completely firm. Break into pieces and store in an airtight container (in refrigerator if the weather is hot).

Smoky & Salty Roasted Nuts

If you usually can't stop after eating a few nuts, you had better keep away from these bad beauties. Rich, smoky, and a little salty, if you aren't careful, a little taste can turn into "where did those nuts go?" in a matter of minutes!

MAKES 3 CUPS (750 ML)
Preparation time: 5 minutes
Cooking time: 30 minutes +
1 hour cooling

2 tbsp soy sauce

2 tbsp toasted sesame oil

2 tsp liquid smoke

2 tsp smoked paprika

1 tsp maple syrup

1 tsp ground white pepper

½ tsp salt

3 cups (750 mL) whole raw nuts, shelled (cashews, almonds, hazelnuts)

salt and ground black pepper, to taste

Preheat oven to 350°F (180°C). Line a large baking sheet with parchment paper.

In a large ziplock plastic bag, combine soy sauce, oil, liquid smoke, paprika, syrup, white pepper, and salt. Add nuts and mix well. Scrunch up bag to thoroughly coat nuts.

Spread nuts in a single layer on baking sheet. Bake for 30 minutes, turning twice, until nuts are browned and all liquid evaporated. A little liquid may burn on parchment paper. Transfer hot nuts to a clean, dry kitchen towel to absorb excess oil. Cool to room temperature, about 1 hour. Taste and season as desired.

Spicy Caramelized Pecans

Perfect as a snack before your backyard barbecue or tossed on a green salad, these are nuts no one can say no to. You may want to make a double batch so there's enough for another day!

MAKES ¾ CUP (185 ML)
Preparation time: 20 minutes + 15 minutes cooling

½ tsp ground cumin
¼ tsp salt
¼ tsp ground black pepper
pinch cayenne pepper, to taste
¾ cup (185 mL) pecans, roughly chopped
⅓ cup (80 mL) light brown sugar

Line a large baking sheet with parchment paper.

In a medium bowl, combine cumin, salt, pepper, and cayenne.

In a small frying pan on medium heat, toast pecans for 5 minutes, until just lightly browned. Remove from pan and toss in spice mixture. Set aside.

In same pan, heat sugar on medium-high heat, stirring continuously, until melted. Remove from heat, add spiced nuts, and continue stirring until nuts are well coated.

Pour mixture onto baking sheet and cool. After about 15 minutes, break into individual nut pieces.

Pumpkin & Corn Cakes

These little morsels are really lovely—a little spicy from the chili powder, a little crunchy from the just-cooked vegetables, a little smooth from the pumpkin purée—all bound together in a Mexican masa harina dough. They are superb when served topped with Melon & Corn Salsa (p. 75) or Fresh Tomato & Pepper Salsa (p. 76). These cakes are equally at home on a bed of salad greens.

MAKES 6–8 SERVINGS

Preparation time: 20 minutes + 1 hour chilling
Cooking time: 10 minutes

1 tbsp olive oil

2 garlic cloves, minced

½ medium onion, finely chopped

½ cup (125 mL) finely chopped green bell peppers, about ½ pepper

1 tsp ground cumin

1 tsp salt

½ tsp ancho chili powder (see p. 250)

½ tsp chipotle chili powder (see p. 250)

¾ cup (185 mL) fresh corn kernels (1 cob), or thawed frozen, or drained and rinsed canned corn

¼ cup (60 mL) finely chopped cilantro

¾ cup (185 mL) canned pumpkin purée (not pie filling)

½ cup (125 mL) masa harina (see p. 251)

¼ cup (60 mL) chickpea flour, sifted if lumpy (see p. 251)

2–3 tbsp olive oil

In a large frying pan on medium, heat 1 tbsp olive oil. Add garlic. When it begins to sizzle, add onions and green bell peppers. Sauté for 5 minutes, until soft.

Stir in cumin, salt, and ancho and chipotle powders and sauté 1 minute more. Stir in corn and cilantro.

Remove from heat, stir in pumpkin purée, masa harina, and chickpea flour until combined well.

Line a small baking sheet or large plate with parchment paper. With dampened hands, form mixture into heaped tbsp-sized balls, flatten to 2-in (5-cm) patties, and place on prepared sheet. Chill in refrigerator for 1 hour.

Wipe down frying pan. On medium, heat 2–3 tbsp oil. Add patties and fry for 3–5 minutes per side, until golden brown with darker patches.

South American Sushi

Just when you thought you knew sushi was just sushi, I jazz it up with some Latin elements. Loaded with protein from two South American grains, this is perfect as a starter at an outdoor party or as a light picnic lunch served with a simple green salad or Smoky Soba Noodle Salad (p. 137). The amaranth is sticky and helps hold the quinoa together; without it, the sushi is hard to roll.

MAKES 6–8 SERVINGS
Preparation time: 45 minutes

3 cups (750 mL) vegetable stock

1 cup (250 mL) quinoa, rinsed

½ cup (125 mL) amaranth, rinsed (see p. 250)

1½ tbsp seasoned rice wine vinegar

1 tbsp agave (see p. 250)

1 tbsp lime juice

4 sheets toasted nori (see p. 251)

FILLINGS

(use in combination or 1 at a time):

1 avocado, thinly sliced

1 jicama, sliced into matchsticks

1 red bell pepper, thinly sliced

1 cucumber, thinly sliced (peeling optional)

1 carrot, thinly sliced

¼ cup (60 mL) green beans, thinly sliced

¼ cup (60 mL) corn kernels

2 tbsp soy sauce, for dipping (optional)

prepared wasabi to taste, optional

....

In a medium saucepan on high heat, bring stock to a boil. Stir in quinoa and amaranth, reduce heat to medium low, and cover. Simmer for 20 minutes, until liquid is absorbed and grains are tender.

Spread cooked grains on baking sheet or large plate to cool to room temperature, about 10 minutes. Turn after 5 minutes.

Return grains to saucepan. Stir in vinegar, agave, and lime juice. Mix well to ensure grains are coated.

Place a sushi mat on a flat surface, with slats horizontal to your position. Place 1 sheet of nori on mat, shiny side down. With a damp rubber spatula, evenly spread ¾ cup (185 mL) seasoned grains over nori. Leave 1-in (2.5-cm) space at end furthest from you. About 1-in (2.5-cm) from edge closest to you, arrange ¼ cup (60 mL) filling in a row along length of grains.

Dampen exposed edge of nori with a little water. Roll sushi from bottom up, away from you, using mat to guide and keep roll tight. Gently press to seal dampened nori. Repeat with 3 remaining nori sheets and remainder of grains and fillings.

With a serrated knife rinsed under hot water as required, slice off raggedy ends, then slice rolled sushi into 1-in (2.5-cm) pieces.

Serve at room temperature with soy sauce and wasabi.

Sushi mats are available in the Asian-food aisle of well-stocked supermarkets, at Asian super-markets, and kitchen-supply stores.

Zesty Broccoli Parcels

This is such a simple and impressive yet tasty way to serve broccoli. Anything en croute always looks like you've spent a lot of time and effort on it. Even your broccoli-hating family and friends will enjoy these delicious parcels that make a perfect al fresco appetizer.

MAKES 9 SERVINGS
Preparation time: 5 minutes
Cooking time: 30 minutes

 (pastry only)

1 tsp olive oil
½ cup (125 mL) finely chopped onions
1½ cups (375 mL) very finely chopped cooked broccoli (stalks and florets), about 8 oz (230 g)
⅓ cup (80 mL) vegan cream cheese
½ tsp orange zest
½ tsp ground nutmeg
salt and ground black pepper, to taste
14 oz (400 g) vegan puff pastry, thawed (see p. 251)

Preheat oven to 400°F (200°C). Line a large baking sheet with parchment paper.

In a small frying pan on medium-high, heat oil. Sauté onions for about 5 minutes, until lightly browned. Remove from heat and cool for 5 minutes.

Add cooked broccoli, cream cheese, orange zest, and nutmeg to pan and mix well. Taste and season as desired, then set aside while you prepare pastry.

On a lightly floured board, roll pastry out to 15-in (38-cm) square, about ¼-in (6-mm) thick. Cut pastry into 9 5-in (12-cm) squares (3 columns, 3 rows). In middle of each, place 2 tbsp filling just off-center, ½-in (1-cm) away from edges. Fold pastry over filling to form a rectangle 5-in (12-cm) long and 2½-in (6.35-cm) wide. Using tines of fork, seal three edges by pressing down ½-in (1-cm) from each edge.

Place pastry parcels on prepared sheet and poke twice with fork to create steam vents. Bake for about 20 minutes, until lightly golden and crispy. Cool on sheet for 5 minutes then transfer to a rack to complete cooling, or serve hot.

Mini-Zesty Broccoli Parcels
Make smaller versions that are 3-in (8-cm) square, and use 1 generous tbsp filling to yield 15 parcels. Bake for 15 minutes.

Twice-Fried Seitan Bites

Apparently, "these are just like popcorn shrimp, but, you know, without the shrimp." These bite-sized, chewy nuggets are wonderful piled high on a plate with a dipping sauce, sprinkled over a salad, served alongside fries as a main, or made into a Pita Po' Boy sandwich (p. 104). They taste great either hot (though they're less this way), or cold (hence great for a picnic).

MAKES 6–8 SERVINGS
Preparation time: 45 minutes, including first frying
Cooking time: 20 minutes

¼ cup (60 mL) nutritional yeast (see p. 251)

1 cup (250 mL) vital wheat gluten powder (see p. 252)

¼ tsp salt

¼ tsp paprika

½ tsp ground cumin

½ tsp onion powder

½ tsp garlic powder

2 tbsp chickpea flour (see p. 251)

1 cup (250 mL) cold vegetable stock

¼ tsp tomato paste

¼ tsp liquid smoke

¾ cup (185 mL) all-purpose flour

¼ tsp salt

¼ tsp ground black pepper

¼ tsp paprika

¼ tsp onion powder

¼ tsp garlic powder

canola oil, enough to ensure depth of at least 2 in (5 cm)

¾ cup (185 mL) plain soy milk

1 tbsp apple cider vinegar

1 tbsp lemon juice

¼ cup (60 mL) vegan sour cream such as Cheater Sour Cream (p. 23)

½ cup (125 mL) fine cornmeal

¼ tsp smoked paprika

¼ tsp ground cumin

¼ tsp dried oregano

⅛–¼ tsp cayenne pepper, to taste

salt and ground black pepper, to taste

In a medium bowl, combine nutritional yeast, vital wheat gluten, salt, paprika, cumin, onion and garlic powder, and chickpea flour. Whisk to eliminate lumps.

In another bowl, whisk together stock, tomato paste, and liquid smoke.

Add stock mixture to dry ingredients and mix well. (It will be quite damp.)

Knead for 3–4 minutes either in bowl or on clean countertop to activate gluten. Let dough (now raw seitan) rest for 5 minutes.

In a medium bowl, combine all-purpose flour, salt, pepper, paprika, and onion and garlic powder.

In a large soup pot on high, heat at least 2-in (5-cm) oil to 350°F (180°C) or use a deep-fryer. Use a frying thermometer to check temperature. Reduce heat to medium to maintain temperature. As oil heats, place paper towels or clean brown paper bags on a cooling rack to drain the seitan once fried.

Oil is ready if a small piece of seitan dough sizzles immediately when dropped into oil.

With a serrated knife, cut seitan dough into ½-in (1-cm) pieces; these will expand as they cook. Toss in flour mixture to coat and keep pieces separate. Shake off excess flour from seitan. Set flour aside.

With tongs or a slotted spoon, carefully add seitan pieces to hot oil, about ¼ at a time. Do not overcrowd pot. *Caution*: Be careful around hot oil!

Fry on 1 side for 3–4 minutes, until golden brown, then turn using tongs or a slotted spoon. Once completely golden and puffy, use tongs or a slotted spoon to remove seitan from oil. Drain on paper towels. Turn off heat under oil.

Cool seitan for 5–10 minutes until cool to the touch. Seitan pieces will deflate slightly as they cool. (If not serving immediately, store in refrigerator for up to 5 days.)

Reheat oil to 350°F (180°C).

In a large bowl, whisk together soy milk, vinegar, lemon juice, and sour cream.

Add fine cornmeal, smoked paprika, cumin, oregano, and cayenne to leftover seasoned flour and mix to combine well.

Dip each piece of seitan in soy milk mixture, then in fine cornmeal/flour mixture. Use 1 hand for wet dip and 1 for dry.

With tongs or a slotted spoon, carefully return seitan to hot oil. Do not overcrowd the pot. Fry on 1 side for 3–4 minutes, until golden brown and crispy. With tongs or slotted spoon, turn and fry other side.

Once completely golden, use tongs or a slotted spoon to remove seitan pieces from oil and drain on paper towels. While still hot, sprinkle with a little salt and pepper, if desired.

Try one of these mayo-based dipping sauces: 1001 Islands Dressing (p. 112); Tartar Sauce (variation, p. 85); or the Po' Boy Mayo (p. 104). For a non-mayo approach, try the Spicy Peanut Sauce (p. 173) or Garlic Dipping Sauce (p. 55).

For more information on seitan, see p. 252.

Mini-Quiches

Before I developed this recipe, I had always made vegan quiche with tofu, but I wanted to try it without; I was pleased with the resulting texture and taste. Use the additional filling suggestions below or get creative with your own. You can prepare this recipe with or without a crust, as they firm up and hold their shape well. Served hot or cold, they are ideal for an outdoor brunch. Note: Soak cashews overnight before preparing recipe.

**MAKES 12 QUICHES,
ABOUT 4 SERVINGS**

Preparation time: 15 minutes

Cooking time: 30 minutes

g (crust only, if used)

n

12 unbaked mini-pie crusts (no larger than muffin-pan size), store-bought or home-made (optional)

½ cup (125 mL) raw cashews, soaked overnight, then drained and rinsed

1 cup (250 mL) ground almonds

¾ cup (185 mL) almond milk

2 tbsp nutritional yeast (see p. 251)

3 tbsp cornstarch

1 tsp prepared yellow mustard

½ tsp salt

¼ tsp ground black pepper

½ tsp dried thyme

½ tsp dried oregano

1 cup (250 mL) fillings (optional) (see p. 39)

Heat oven to 375°F (190°C). If making crustless quiches, spray a muffin pan with non-stick spray or lightly oil. If using pie crusts, have 12 mini-pie crusts ready.

In a blender or food processor, blend soaked cashews to a smooth paste, scraping down sides of bowl as required. Add ground almonds and milk and process until completely smooth and combined well. Add nutritional yeast, cornstarch, mustard, salt, pepper, thyme, and oregano. Blend to combine well.

Transfer mixture to a large bowl. Stir in additional fillings (see following page), if desired. Spoon mixture into prepared muffin pans or pastry crusts. Smooth tops.

Bake for 25–30 minutes, until crusts are golden and filling is firm to the touch. Cool in pan for 5 minutes.

Fillings

Quiche Lorraine
¾ cup (185 mL) tofu, tempeh (see p. 252), or coconut vegan bacon and ¼ cup (60 mL) grated vegan cheese.

Peas & ham
½ cup (125 mL) thawed frozen peas and ½ cup (125 mL) finely chopped commercial vegan ham.

Poached garlic & broccoli
1 cup (250 mL) finely chopped cooked broccoli (stalks and florets) and 3 cloves Stovetop Poached Garlic (p. 21).

Roasted red bell pepper
1 cup (250 mL) finely chopped roasted red bell peppers.

Asparagus
1 cup (250 mL) roasted or blanched, finely chopped asparagus spears.

Mushroom
In a small frying pan on medium heat, melt 1 tbsp vegan margarine. Sauté 1½ cups (375 mL) finely sliced mushrooms with 2 garlic cloves for about 5 minutes. Toss with 1 tbsp minced chives.

Basil & sun-dried tomato
½ cup (125 mL) finely chopped sun-dried tomatoes (do not reconstitute) and ½ cup (125 mL) shredded fresh basil.

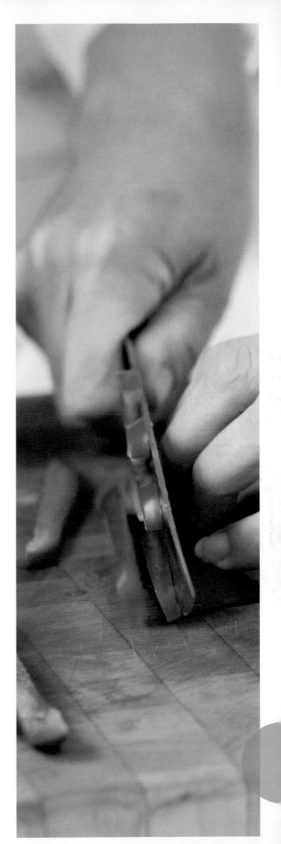

Tomato & Olive Tarts

These quiche-like tarts are both gluten- and soy-free and have a wonderful creamy, smooth texture. Although heavier than a "regular" quiche, they are a delight to eat either hot or cold. Serve with a salad for a perfect al fresco lunch or dinner. These are just as good, if not better, the next day, so leftovers (if you have any) are a good thing!

MAKES 3–6 SERVINGS
Preparation time: 10 minutes
Cooking time: 20 minutes

1 cup (250 mL) raw cashews, soaked overnight, then drained and rinsed
¼ cup (60 mL) almond milk
¼ cup (60 mL) olive oil
¼ cup (60 mL) chickpea flour (see p. 251)
2 tbsp tapioca starch or cornstarch
1 tbsp nutritional yeast (see p. 251)
½ tsp salt
½ tsp ground dry mustard
⅛ tsp ground black pepper
½ cup (125 mL) finely chopped olives (black, green, kalamata, or combination)
¼ cup (60 mL) finely chopped sun-dried tomatoes
1–2 ripe Roma tomatoes, thinly sliced

Preheat oven to 400°F (200°C). Lightly oil a 6-cup muffin pan.

In a food processor, combine cashews, milk, oil, flour, tapioca starch, nutritional yeast, salt, dry mustard, and pepper. Blend until very smooth and creamy. Stop and scrape down sides of bowl as required.

Add olives and sun-dried tomatoes and pulse once or twice to combine.

Scrape filling into prepared muffin pans and smooth tops. Garnish with fresh tomato slices.

Bake for 20–25 minutes, until filling is firm to a light touch and top is golden.

Cool in pans for at least 15 minutes before serving.

Slow Cooker Tomatillo & Tomato Tamales

This is a bit of an epic recipe, so choose a day when you have time to devote to the kitchen. I like to serve these with Fresh Tomato & Pepper Salsa (p. 76) or a simple tomato sauce. Remember to unwrap the corn husks before eating!

MAKES 18–20 TAMALES OR 6–8 SERVINGS

Preparation time: 1 hour & 20 minutes
Cooking time: 5 hours

35 large corn husks

FILLING

6–8 medium tomatillos, washed, peeled, and halved
2 serrano chili peppers, halved and seeded
1 tbsp olive oil
2 garlic cloves, minced
1½ tsp cumin seeds
1 medium onion, finely chopped
2 cups (500 mL) finely chopped peeled white potatoes
½ tsp salt
2 Roma tomatoes, seeded and finely chopped
salt and ground black pepper, to taste

MASA DOUGH

¾ cup (185 mL) vegan shortening
¼ cup (60 mL) soft coconut oil at room temperature
1 tsp onion powder
1 tsp garlic powder
½ tsp smoked paprika
½ tsp salt
3 cups (750 mL) masa harina (see p. 251)
2½ cups (625 mL) warm vegetable stock

Corn husks

Sort through corn husks to remove debris and dirt. Use large ones for easy wrapping; save smaller ones to tear into strips for tying.

In a large bowl, soak corn husks in warm water, until soft and pliable. Set a heavy item such as a saucepan lid on top of husks to keep husks submerged.

Soak for about 1 hour.

Peel 2–3 husks into ¼- to ½-in (6-mm to 1-cm) wide strips to use as ties, as required (2 ties per tamale).

Prepare filling

Preheat oven broiler to high.

On a lightly oiled baking sheet, broil tomatillos and chili peppers, cut sides down, for about 10 minutes, until skins are charred and juice is bursting out. Cool for 10 minutes, until easily handled, then peel off blackened skins. Mince chili peppers and roughly chop tomatillos.

In a large frying pan on medium, heat oil. Add garlic and cumin seeds and allow to sizzle. Add onions and sauté for 5 minutes, until translucent. Add potatoes and salt and sauté for 5 minutes. Add roasted tomatillos, chilies, and 2 tbsp water. Sauté for 20–25 minutes, until potatoes are completely tender and liquid has reduced. Potatoes and onions will be slightly caramelized.

Add tomatoes and stir to combine well. The mixture will look thick. Taste and season as desired. Set aside while you prepare the dough.

Prepare dough

In a large bowl, cream shortening and coconut oil for 7–10 minutes until very light and fluffy. The more you cream, the better texture the tamales will have. (Microwave in 10-second bursts to soften coconut oil if too firm to cream.) Add onion powder, garlic powder, paprika, and salt, and cream until combined well.

In another large bowl, combine masa harina with warm stock. Mix well to eliminate lumps.

Transfer masa mix to bowl with creamed mixture and beat for 5–7 minutes, until combined well. Dough should be smooth and yet light. It will look and feel a little like smooth mashed potato or play-dough.

Cover dough with a damp kitchen towel or soaked corn husk to prevent drying out.

Make tamales

Place a collapsible vegetable steamer basket in a slow cooker. Add ¾ cup (185 mL) water, just enough to reach bottom of basket. Line bottom and sides of steamer insert and sides of slow cooker with 5 or 6 soaked corn husks to prevent tamales from directly touching sides of slow cooker.

Place a clean tea towel on a flat surface. Keep a few clean towels as backups if first becomes too wet.

Lay a soaked husk on towel, with broad end nearest you. Place a generous 3 tbsp dough onto husk. Keep remaining dough covered.

Spread dough over husk to form a 3 x 5-in (8 x 12-cm) rectangle, leaving a space of about 4 in (10 cm) down from narrow end of husk and about 2 in (5 cm) up from wide end.

Spread dough to the edge of 1 long side and at least 2 in (5 cm) from the other long side. Try to keep dough about ¼-in (6-mm) thick.

Spread about 1½ tbsp filling vertically down center of dough.

Fold over long side of corn husk without masa dough to meet other edge of dough, to cover filling. Wrap 2 in (5 cm) spare edge of corn husk around back of tamale, sealing in dough.

Fold broad end up and over bottom of tamale. Tie securely with prepared strip of corn husk or use kitchen twine. Fold longer narrow end down and tie.

Repeat with remaining husks, dough, and filling.

In the steamer basket inside slow cooker, stack wrapped and tied tamales (upright if possible), as they are made.

Cover, set heat to high, and cook for 5–5½ hours, until tamales are tender. Once done, corn husk will peel easily off dough.

Start soaking corn husks before chopping vegetables. While corn husks soak for about 1 hour and tomatillos and chilies roast, chop onions and garlic. Chop potatoes while onions sauté. Prepare dough while potatoes cook.

You can make filling in advance and store in refrigerator for up to 3 days.

Once cooked and cooled, freeze tamales (in husks) in a single layer. When frozen, bag into meal portions for quick reheated suppers "on the go." Microwave from frozen for about 4 minutes on high to reheat.

Mini-Spring Rolls with Chili Lime Dipping Sauce

You won't believe how authentic these taste or how easy they are to make, and even if they're a little time-consuming, the end results are well worth the effort. Serve them at your next outdoor party with dipping sauce on the side.

MAKES 8–10 SERVINGS
Preparation time: 40 minutes
Cooking time: 20 minutes

 (pastry only)

CHILI LIME DIPPING SAUCE

This sauce is thin, not sticky, so it soaks into the outer layer of the crisp wrapper and gives a burst of hot, sweet, and sour to spring rolls.

¼ cup (60 mL) fresh lime juice
3 tbsp Thai sweet chili sauce (see p. 252)
2 tbsp soy sauce
1 tbsp brown rice syrup (see p. 250)
1 tbsp rice wine vinegar
1 tsp Asian-style hot sauce, such as Sriracha
½ tsp garlic powder

In a small bowl, whisk to combine all ingredients. Chill for at least 1 hour in refrigerator before serving.

FILLING & WRAPPERS

If your pan is not large enough to cook filling all at once, complete in batches.

¾ cup (185 mL) TVP granules (see p. 252)
1 cup (250 mL) boiling vegetable stock
1 tbsp soy sauce
1 tbsp canola oil
½ tsp ground cumin
1 tsp Chinese five-spice powder
2 garlic cloves, minced
1 tbsp minced fresh ginger
½ onion, finely sliced
3 cups (750 mL) shredded cabbage
3 cups (750 mL) mung bean sprouts
½ cup (125 mL) shredded carrots
¼ cup (60 mL) thinly bias-cut spring onions
¼ cup (60 mL) thinly sliced green bell peppers
50 (1 packet) 5-in (12-cm) square vegan spring roll wrappers (see p. 252)
canola oil, enough to ensure depth of at least 2 in (5 cm)

In a medium bowl, combine TVP, stock, and soy sauce. Cover for 10 minutes to reconstitute.

In a large frying pan on medium, heat oil. Stir in ground spices, garlic, and ginger, and allow to sizzle.

Stir in onions and sauté for 3–4 minutes, until just until soft. Stir in TVP mixture and sauté for 2–3 minutes.

Stir in cabbage, bean sprouts, carrots, spring onions, and bell peppers. Sauté for 2–3 minutes, until just tender. (Vegetables should have a bright color.) Remove from heat and cool for 5 minutes.

In a large soup pot on high, heat 2 in (5 cm) oil to 375°F (190°C) or use a deep-fryer. Use a frying thermometer to check temperature. Reduce heat to medium to maintain temperature. Oil is ready if a small piece of wrapper sizzles immediately when dropped in.

Place paper towels or clean brown paper bags on a cooling rack to drain rolls once fried.

Assemble & cook spring rolls

Place 1 tbsp filling in the middle of each wrapper, slightly toward the bottom end. Fold sides in to partially cover filling, then roll wrapper up away from you, to create a cigar-shaped roll. Seal edges with a little water.

Place completed rolls aside until all are filled.

Once oil is to temperature, use tongs or a slotted spoon to add 8–10 rolls to pot. Do not overcrowd the pot. *Caution*: Be careful around hot oil!

If any rolls burst open, remove from oil immediately.

Fry 1 side for 3–4 minutes, until golden brown. With tongs or a slotted spoon, turn and cook other side.

Once completely golden, use tongs or a slotted spoon to remove from oil. Drain on paper towels.

Allow oil to return to 375°F (190°C) before cooking further batches.

Asian supermarkets usually carry vegan spring roll wrappers, which may be sold frozen. They're made from wheat flour, water, coconut oil, and salt. Keep thawed wrappers covered with a damp cloth if not using immediately so they stay flexible and don't dry out.

Chinese five-spice powder is equal parts ground Szechuan or black pepper, ground star anise (or ground anise and a pinch of allspice), and ground cinnamon, cloves, and fennel seeds.

Samosa Spring Rolls

Asian fusion, baby! I've taken an Indian-inspired samosa filling and wrapped it in Chinese-style spring roll wrappers, then deep-fried them. Serve with the GuacaRaita (p. 59) or Garlic Dipping Sauce (p. 55) for a cooling sauce option, or if you'd like to up the heat, try the Chili Lime Dipping Sauce (p. 45).

MAKES 8–10 SERVINGS

Preparation time: 35 minutes
Cooking time: 20 minutes, but this varies

 (pastry only)

1 tbsp canola oil

2 tsp cumin seeds

2 tsp mustard seeds

1 tsp crushed coriander seeds

1 tsp ground cumin

2 tsp curry powder, your choice of heat

¼ to ½ tsp chili flakes (optional)

3 garlic cloves, minced

2 tbsp minced fresh ginger

1 onion, finely chopped

2 cups (500 mL) cubed yellow-fleshed potatoes, such as Yukon gold (peeling optional)

2 cups (500 mL) peeled, diced carrots

1½ cups (375 mL) canned coconut milk, or 1 14-oz (398-mL) can

1 cup (250 mL) thawed frozen green peas

¼ cup (60 mL) golden raisins

salt and ground black pepper, to taste

50 (1 packet) 5-in (12-cm) square vegan spring roll wrappers (see p. 252)

canola oil, enough to ensure depth of at least 2 in (5 cm)

In a large frying pan on medium, heat oil. Stir in cumin, mustard, and coriander seeds and allow to sizzle for 1 minute. Stir in ground cumin, curry powder, and chili flakes and sauté for 1 minute. Stir in garlic and ginger and allow to sizzle.

Stir in onions and sauté for 3–4 minutes, until soft. Stir in potatoes and carrots and sauté for 5 minutes, until just soft. Stir in coconut milk. Cover pan and cook for 7 minutes, until potatoes are tender and coconut milk has thickened and reduced.

Stir in green peas and raisins. Cook, uncovered, for a further 2–3 minutes until peas are tender. Remove from heat. Taste and season as desired, then allow to cool for 20 minutes or until room temperature.

In a large soup pot on high, heat 2 in (5 cm) oil to 375°F (190°C) or use a deep fryer. Use a frying thermometer to check temperature. Reduce heat to medium to maintain temperature. Oil is ready when a small piece of wrapper sizzles immediately when dropped in.

Place paper towels or clean brown paper bags on a cooling rack to drain rolls once fried.

Assemble & cook spring rolls

Place 1 tbsp filling in the middle of each wrapper, slightly toward the bottom end. Fold sides in to cover filling, then roll wrapper up, away from you, to create a cigar-shaped roll. Seal edges with a little water.

Place completed rolls aside until all are filled.

Once oil is to temperature, use tongs or a slotted spoon to carefully add rolls to hot oil, 8–10 at a time. *Caution*: Be careful around hot oil! Do not overcrowd pot.

If any rolls burst open, remove from oil immediately.

Fry 1 side for 3–4 minutes, until golden brown. With tongs or a slotted spoon turn to cook other side.

Once completely golden, use tongs or a slotted spoon to remove rolls from oil. Drain on paper towels.

Allow oil to return to 375°F (190°C) before cooking further batches.

Cider-Battered Tofu

I have fond (pre-vegan) childhood memories of sitting outside on a hot New Zealand summer evening, overlooking the ocean and gobbling up fish and chips out of a newspaper packet. The fish was crispy and hot, overly salty, and doused in tomato sauce (ketchup). This recipe takes me right back, especially if I eat it outside—even more if I'm near the ocean. Serve with thick-cut fries wrapped in parchment paper, then in newspaper for a from-the-chippie feel.

MAKES 4–6 SERVINGS

Preparation time: 10 minutes + 1 hour marinating

Cooking time: 30 minutes

1 lb (500 g) extra-firm regular tofu (water-packed), drained and pressed

MARINADE

3 tbsp lime juice

1 tbsp soy sauce

1 tsp lime zest

2 garlic cloves, minced

1 Serrano chili pepper, minced

canola oil, enough to ensure depth of at least 2 in (5 cm)

½ cup (125 mL) all-purpose flour

BATTER

1 cup (250 mL) + 2 tbsp all-purpose flour

¼ cup (60 mL) + 2 tbsp fine cornmeal

1½ tsp baking powder

½ tsp baking soda

½ tsp salt

¼ tsp ground black pepper

¼ tsp garlic powder

¼ tsp onion powder

1¾ (415 mL) cups + 2 tbsp cold dry cider, not quite 1 large can

salt and ground black pepper, to taste

Once tofu is pressed, cut widthwise into 12 rectangles. Cut these corner to corner to create 24 triangles.

Combine lime juice, soy sauce, lime zest, garlic, and chili in a large flat container with a resealable lid or in a large ziplock bag. Add tofu triangles and toss to coat. Rub marinade onto each piece through bag. Marinate in refrigerator for at least 1 hour (longer is better), turning after 30 minutes.

In a large soup pot on high, heat at least 2 in (5 cm) oil to 375°F (190°C) or use a deep fryer. Use a frying thermometer to check temperature. Reduce heat to medium to maintain it at temperature. Oil is ready when a small piece of tofu sizzles immediately when dropped in.

Place paper towels or clean brown paper bags on a cooling rack to drain tofu once fried.

On a large plate or platter, spread ½ cup (125 mL) all-purpose flour.

In a large bowl, whisk flour, cornmeal, baking powder, baking soda, salt, pepper, garlic powder, and onion powder. Make a well in center of dry ingredients.

Remove tofu pieces from marinade and toss to coat in plain flour.

Add leftover marinade and cider to well in dry ingredients mixture, ¼ cup (60 mL) at a time. Whisk to combine until a smooth batter is formed.

Once oil is to temperature, remove tofu from plain flour and coat in batter. Be generous—there is enough for a good coating. Carefully add 4–6 tofu pieces to hot oil, taking care not to splash oil. *Caution*: Be careful around hot oil!

Fry on 1 side for 3–4 minutes, until golden brown. With tongs or a slotted spoon, turn and cook other side.

Once completely golden, use tongs or slotted spoon to remove tofu from oil. Drain on paper towels.

Sprinkle with a little salt and pepper while still hot.

Allow oil to return to 375°F (190°C) between batches. Remove any batter droppings between batches.

This is my spin on beer-battered tofu, using cider instead. The recipe can be successfully made with beer or soda water. Cider (or beer or soda water) should be cold for best results. *Note*: Use dry, not sweet, cider.

Leftover batter? I use mine to coat slices of ripe plantain or avocado, then deep-fry them—so good!

THESE OFT-FORGOTTEN ELEMENTS *can elevate a simple vegan burger (even store-bought ones) to something approaching gourmet. Many of the dips and sauces that follow are cool and refreshing, others are spicy and heating, others still acidic and sharp—but all are tasty and good. I offer suggestions throughout the book on where to use these recipes, but they are, by nature, mix-and-match, so feel free to use as you wish!*

dips, sauces, condiments & accompaniments

Crudités (and other great dippers)

Here are some useful ideas for what to serve alongside all the wonderful dips that follow. Crudités translates as cut raw vegetables, but the ideas don't stop there.

Veggies

- asparagus spears, raw or lightly steamed
- beets, peeled and cut into 2–3-in (5–8-cm) long sticks
- broccoli florets
- Brussels sprouts, lightly steamed or roasted, quartered
- carrots, peeled and cut into 2–3-in (5–8-cm) long sticks or "baby" carrots
- cauliflower florets
- celery stalks, cut into 2–3-in (5–8-cm) long sticks
- cherry tomatoes on skewers or toothpicks
- cucumbers, cut into 2–3-in (5–8-cm) long sticks, peeling and seeding optional
- endive leaves
- fennel bulb, cut into strips 2–3-in (5–8-cm) long; lightly squeeze a lemon over them to prevent discoloration
- gherkins or pickles
- green beans, trimmed
- spring onions, trimmed
- jicama, peeled and cut into 2–3-in (5–8-cm) long sticks; lightly squeeze a lime over them to prevent discoloration
- kale leaves, trimmed to remove hard centers
- mushrooms, quartered
- radishes
- red (or green or yellow) peppers, cut into 2–3-in (5–8-cm) long strips
- snow or snap peas
- zucchinis, cut into 2–3-in (5–8-cm) long strips

Other dippers

- baguette slices
- baked root vegetable chips
- breadsticks, store-bought or home-made, such as Garlic Breadsticks (p. 185)
- canned hearts of palm
- corn chips
- crackers, store-bought or home-made, such as Nut & Seed Crackers (p. 183) or Gluten-free Corn Crackers (p. 184)
- Fu'Tons (p. 122) or tofu cubes on skewers or toothpicks
- mini-rice crackers
- pita bread triangles
- pickles
- potato chips
- potato wedges or oven fries, such as Spiced Oven Potato Wedges (p. 174)
- pretzels, soft or hard
- vegan cheese cubes
- vegan deli meat slices

Garlic Dipping Sauce

This is my favorite sauce for dipping grilled vegetables, though it's not just for veggies; it's also wonderful alongside a simply grilled piece of tofu or nice crusty bread. I've also enjoyed it with the Cedar Planked Rosemary & Lemon Tofu (p. 164).

MAKES ¾ CUP (185 ML)

Preparation time: 15 minutes, not including making the Stovetop Poached Garlic

n

½ recipe Stovetop Poached Garlic & Garlic Oil (p. 21): ¼ cup (60 mL) oil and 11 garlic cloves

½ cup (125 mL) ground almonds

¼ cup (60 mL) Dry Chees-y Mix (p. 18)

½ cup (125 mL) almond milk

½ tsp salt

¼ tsp ground black pepper

salt and ground black pepper, to taste

In a blender or food processor, combine garlic, oil, almonds, Chees-y Mix, milk, salt, and pepper. Process until smooth and creamy.

Transfer to a small saucepan on medium heat. Stirring frequently, cook for 5–7 minutes, until thickened.

Taste and season as desired. If sauce curdles, whisk briefly to re-emulsify.

Quick Tahini Falafel Sauce

This sauce is perfect with the Aussie Falafel (p. 102), either drizzled over top or as a dipping sauce. Most tahini sauces for falafel are made with yogurt, but here I use sour cream for its creaminess and thickness. There's no reason to limit this to falafel; use it as a multi-purpose dipping sauce, on vegetables, or even as a salad dressing. This sauce thickens a lot in the refrigerator, so add more water as required before serving.

MAKES ½ CUP (125 ML)
Preparation time: 5 minutes

2 tbsp tahini (see p. 252)
1 tbsp olive oil
1 tbsp lemon juice
3 tbsp vegan sour cream such as Cheater Sour Cream (p. 23)
salt and ground black pepper, to taste

In a small bowl, combine tahini, oil, and lemon juice until smooth. Stir in sour cream until combined well. Stir in 3 tbsp water, 1 tbsp at a time. If necessary, add more until desired thickness is reached.

Taste and season as desired.

Cover and store for up to 5 days in refrigerator.

Asian-Inspired Sesame & Cilantro Dip

Thick, rich, and creamy with no packet mix in sight! This dip sings with Asian-influenced flavors and is great with raw vegetables, chips, and crackers. Perfect paired with drinks on the deck.

MAKES 1 CUP (250 ML)
Preparation time: *10 minutes +*
1 hour chilling

½ cup (125 mL) vegan sour cream such as Cheater Sour Cream (p. 23)

¼ cup (60 mL) vegan mayonnaise such as Tofonnaise (p.110)

2 tbsp very finely chopped cilantro

1 tbsp sesame seeds

1 tbsp rice wine vinegar

2 tsp toasted sesame oil

2 tsp soy sauce

1 tsp agave (see p. 250)

1 tsp grated fresh ginger

1 garlic clove, minced

¼ tsp chili flakes

salt, ground black pepper and Asian-style hot sauce (such as Sriracha), to taste

1 tsp cilantro leaves, to garnish

In a small serving bowl, combine sour cream, mayonnaise, cilantro, sesame seeds, vinegar, oil, soy sauce, agave, ginger, garlic, and chili flakes. Whisk with a fork to combine.

Taste and season as desired.

Chill for 1 hour before serving. Garnish with cilantro leaves.

Creamy Olive Dip

Not a tapenade-style olive dip, this one is creamy and a little chees-y. It works not only as a dip with crackers but as a thick and chunky salad dressing as well. It's a little on the salty side, so the agave is added for balance, but if you like it that way, you may not need it.

MAKES 1 CUP (250 ML)

Preparation time: *10 minutes + 1 hour chilling*

n *(in Chees-y Mix)*

s

¼ cup (60 mL) vegan mayonnaise such as Tofonnaise (p. 110)

¼ cup (60 mL) vegan sour cream such as Cheater Sour Cream (p. 23)

¼ cup (60 mL) finely chopped black olives

2 tbsp finely chopped green olives

1 tbsp lemon juice

1 tbsp Chees-y Mix (p. 18)

2 tsp finely chopped capers

½ tsp agave (optional) (see p. 250)

salt and ground black pepper, to taste

2 or 3 whole olives, to garnish

In a small bowl, combine mayonnaise, sour cream, olives, lemon juice, Chees-y Mix, capers, and agave, and mix to combine well. Cover and chill for at least 1 hour.

Taste and adjust seasoning as required before serving garnished with whole olives.

I like my green olives stuffed with pimentos, but if you don't, use plain ones or Kalamata olives.

GuacaRaita

Combining the cooling taste of raita, the yogurt-based Middle Eastern dip, and the smooth creaminess of guacamole, this is one very more-ish dip you can feel good about indulging in. The refreshing cucumber and mint complement the rich avocado. Best eaten on the day it's made or the avocado will discolor. Perfect for an outdoor party on a hot summer night.

MAKES 2 CUPS (500 mL)
Preparation time: *10 minutes +*
1 hour chilling

2 ripe avocados, peeled and pitted
¼ cup (60 mL) seeded and finely chopped cucumber (peeling optional)
2 tbsp vegan sour cream such as Cheater Sour Cream (p. 23) (optional)
1½ tbsp lime juice
1½ tbsp finely chopped fresh mint
¼ tsp lime zest
1 shallot, minced
salt and ground black pepper, to taste

In a medium bowl, roughly mash avocados with a potato masher to desired smoothness. Stir in cucumbers, sour cream, lime juice, mint, lime zest, and shallots. Taste and season as desired.

Chill for 1 hour before serving.

Caper & Edamame Dip

The green color of this dip is so intense, you could be forgiven for thinking it's guacamole—until you taste its briny kick. Enjoy with crudités (see suggestions, p. 54); I especially like it paired with celery sticks.

MAKES 1 CUP (250 ML)

Preparation time: *10 minutes + 1 hour chilling*

1 cup (250 mL) frozen edamame, cooked to package directions, refreshed under cold water

¼ cup (60 mL) + 2 tbsp vegan mayonnaise such as Tofonnaise (p. 110)

2 tbsp capers with brine

1 garlic clove, minced

1 shallot, finely chopped

salt, ground black pepper, and caper brine to taste

In a food processor or blender, combine edamame, mayonnaise, capers, garlic, and shallots and blend until smooth. Cover and chill for at least 1 hour.

Taste and season as desired before serving.

Chilled Arugula & Artichoke Dip

The restaurant where my husband once worked served a watercress and artichoke dip—their version of the eternally popular spinach and artichoke dip. Most versions are loaded with cheese, then topped with more cheese and baked. My version uses sharp, bitter arugula as the green, and I've pared the dip back to essential flavors. Serve this cold.

MAKES 1½ CUPS (375 ML)
Preparation Time: *10 minutes + 1 hour chilling*

n *(in the Dry Chees-y Mix)*

s

3 cups (750 mL) packed baby arugula

½ cup (125 mL) canned artichoke hearts, about 3 pieces

¼ cup (60 mL) vegan mayonnaise such as Tofonnaise (p. 110)

¼ cup (60 mL) vegan sour cream such as Cheater Sour Cream (p. 23)

2 tbsp plain soy milk

1 tbsp Dry Chees-y Mix (p. 18)

1 tbsp lemon juice

1 garlic clove, chopped

1 shallot, chopped

salt and ground black pepper, to taste

In a large frying pan on medium heat, wilt arugula in a few drops of water until ⅓ of its original volume.

In a food processor or blender, process all ingredients. This does not need to be totally smooth, so leave some texture. Cover and chill for at least 1 hour.

Taste and season as desired before serving.

White Bean & Peanut Dip

This dip is very peanut-y, so it's not for haters or those with nut allergies. It is quite thick; if overly so, add more water by the teaspoon to thin it out. It's perfect for scooping with crudités or tortilla chips, spread on toast or served over pasta, served alongside a salad, eaten out of the container with a spoon … you get the idea.

MAKES 1½ CUPS (375 ML)
Preparation time: 5 minutes

1 cup (250 mL) cooked cannellini (white kidney) beans (if canned, drain and rinse)

½ cup (125 mL) roasted salted peanuts

2 garlic cloves, roughly chopped

2 tbsp soy sauce

2 tbsp lime juice

1 tbsp smooth, natural peanut butter

1 tbsp Thai sweet chili sauce (see p. 252)

1 tsp grated fresh ginger

salt, ground black pepper, chili flakes, and hot sauce, to taste

1 tbsp finely chopped cilantro to garnish (optional)

In a food processor or powerful blender, blend beans, peanuts, garlic, soy sauce, lime juice, 2 tbsp water, peanut butter, chili sauce, and ginger until as smooth as desired. Taste and season as desired.

Store in refrigerator until ready to serve. Garnish with cilantro.

The dip will thicken if it sits in the refrigerator overnight (it tastes even better the next day, so make it in advance if you are able to); just add more water, and give it another stir before serving.

Oil-free White Bean Hummus

This dip is lusciously creamy, without a drop of oil in sight. I use cannellini beans in addition to the chickpeas to get the super smooth texture and to add layers of tasty hummus goodness.

MAKES 2 CUPS (500 ML)
Preparation time: 10 minutes

1 cup (250 mL) cooked chickpeas (if canned, drain and rinse)

1 cup (250 mL) cooked cannellini (white kidney) beans (if canned, drain and rinse)

3 tbsp tahini (see p. 252)

1 tbsp hemp seeds (optional) (see p. 251)

2 garlic cloves, chopped

2 tbsp lemon juice

2 tbsp nutritional yeast (see p. 251)

1 tbsp finely chopped fresh parsley

½ tsp paprika

½ tsp ground cumin

¼ tsp onion powder

¼ tsp garlic powder

¼ tsp salt

⅛ teaspoon ground black pepper

salt and ground black pepper, to taste

In a blender or food processor, combine chickpeas, cannellini beans, tahini, hemp seeds, garlic, lemon juice, nutritional yeast, parsley, paprika, cumin, onion powder, garlic powder, salt, and pepper. Pulse until smooth.

Add 3–5 tbsp water, 1 tbsp at a time, and pulse to combine, until it reaches desired consistency. Taste and season as desired.

Chipotle & Peanut Butter Hummus (p. 66)

Gluten-free Corn Crackers (p. 184)

Oil-free White Bean Hummus (opposite)

Chipotle & Peanut Butter Hummus

Smoky heat is added to hummus, which is already enhanced by peanut butter. Try this as a dip for raw veggies or nacho chips, on sandwiches or burgers, or as a dollop over a bowl of rice.

MAKES 1½ CUPS (375 ML)
Preparation time: 10 minutes

2 cups (500 mL) cooked chickpeas, or 1 19-oz (540-mL) can, drained and rinsed
2 garlic cloves, roughly chopped
1½ tbsp lemon juice
1½ tbsp lime juice
3 tbsp peanut butter
3 tbsp olive oil
1–2 canned chipotle chilies in adobo, seeded (see p. 250)
¼ tsp ground cumin
salt and ground black pepper, to taste

In a blender or food processor, pulse to combine chickpeas, garlic, lemon juice, lime juice, peanut butter, oil, chipotle, and cumin until combined well. Add 2–4 tbsp water, 1 tbsp at a time, and pulse until smooth. Stop to scrape down sides of bowl as required.

Taste and season as desired.

Tandoori Spiced Hummus

I have a love-love relationship with chickpeas; I can't get enough of them, to the point that one year Santa put some in my stocking. (I'd been a very good girl that year!) The spice mix adds zip to the creaminess of the blended chickpeas—just don't add too much.

MAKES 1 CUP (250 ML)
Preparation time: *5 minutes + 1 hour chilling (optional)*

1 cup (250 mL) cooked chickpeas (if canned, drain and rinse)
1 garlic clove, roughly chopped
1 tbsp tahini (see p. 252)
1 tbsp lemon juice
1 tbsp olive oil
¾ tsp Tandoori Spice Mix (p. 22)
salt and ground black pepper, to taste

In a blender or food processor, blend chickpeas, garlic, 2 tbsp water, tahini, lemon juice, oil, and spice mix until smooth. Stop to scrape down sides of bowl as required.

Taste and season as desired.

Refrigerate for at least 1 hour before serving.

Walnut & Mushroom Pâté (p. 70)

Nut & Seed Crackers (p. 183)

Brandied Tempeh Pâté (opposite)

Brandied Tempeh Pâté

This is a lovely smooth pâté, great for spreading on toast or crostini or with crudités at your next elegant picnic. It's quite decadent tasting, but filled with wholesome ingredients that you can feel good about.

MAKES 1½ CUPS (375 ML)
Preparation time: 5 minutes
Cooking time: 25 minutes + 1 hour chilling

2 tsp apple cider vinegar

1 bay leaf

8 oz (230 g) tempeh (whole piece) (see p. 252)

1 tbsp olive oil

2 garlic cloves, minced

1 shallot, minced

1 tsp Marmite (see p. 251)

1 tbsp tomato paste

1 tsp agave (see p. 250)

½ tsp dried sage

½ tsp dried thyme

½ tsp salt

¼ tsp ground black pepper

¼ cup (60 mL) brandy

3–5 tbsp vegetable stock or water, room temperature

salt and ground black pepper, to taste

In a medium frying pan, bring 2 cups (500 mL) water, vinegar, and bay leaf to a boil. Add tempeh, reduce heat to medium, and cover. Cook for 8 minutes, turn, and cook for another 7 minutes. Remove from heat, discard cooking water, and refresh tempeh under cold water until cool to the touch. Cut tempeh into ½-in (1-cm) cubes. Set aside.

Wipe frying pan clean. On medium-high, heat oil. Sauté garlic and shallots for 2 minutes, until sizzling. Add tempeh and sauté for 3 minutes, until lightly browned. Add Marmite, tomato paste, agave and herbs, salt and pepper, and sauté for 1 minute more.

Transfer mixture to a blender or food processor. Use brandy to deglaze pan, then add to blender. Process, adding stock 1 tbsp at a time, until smooth.

Taste and season as desired.

Transfer to serving dish and chill for at least 1 hour before serving.

Walnut & Mushroom Pâté

This rich pâté is wonderful served as an appetizer for a fancy outdoor party with crudités or squares of whole wheat toast. It is also great spread on delicate "finger" sandwiches as part of a picnic selection.

MAKES 1½ CUPS (375 mL)
Preparation time: 15 minutes
Cooking time: 30 minutes + 30 minutes chilling

1 tbsp olive oil
½ cup (125 mL) finely chopped, onions
1 shallot, finely chopped
2 garlic cloves, minced
3½ cups (830 mL) finely chopped button mushrooms, roughly 8 medium
½ tsp salt
½ tsp dried thyme
½ tsp dried oregano
¼ tsp ground black pepper
¼ cup (60 mL) red wine
1 tsp Marmite (see p. 251)
½ cup (125 mL) walnut pieces
½ cup (125 mL) almond pieces
salt and ground black pepper, to taste

In a medium frying pan on medium, heat oil. Sauté onions, shallots, and garlic for about 5 minutes, until soft. Add mushrooms, salt, thyme, oregano, and pepper and sauté for a further 10 minutes. Add red wine and cook for about 10 minutes, until liquid is nearly all gone. Stir in Marmite. Remove from heat.

In a food processor, pulse nuts to a coarse meal. Add mushroom mixture, and pulse to combine. Taste and season as desired.

Chill for at least 2 hours before serving.

Spicy Peanut Sauce

Is the unlikely event you have leftovers, the sauce will thicken in the refrigerator overnight. I mix the leftover sauce with a little water or mayonnaise to use as a salad dressing. If you want to serve it hot, reheat on low and stir frequently.

MAKES 1 CUP (250 ML)
Preparation time: 5 minutes
Cooking time: 5 minutes

1 tbsp peanut or canola oil
2 garlic cloves, minced
1 tbsp grated fresh ginger
1 tbsp finely chopped cilantro, leaves and stems
2 tbsp Thai sweet chili sauce (see p. 252)
1 tbsp tomato ketchup
1 tbsp rice wine vinegar
¼ cup (60 mL) + 2 tbsp smooth peanut butter

In a medium saucepan on medium, heat oil. Sauté garlic, ginger, and cilantro for about 1 minute. Add ½ cup (125 mL) water, chili sauce, ketchup, and vinegar and bring to a boil.

Remove from heat and stir in peanut butter until smooth and creamy. Return to heat for 3–4 minutes and stir to thicken.

Peanut Butter Adobo Barbecue Sauce

Spicy and creamy with a subtle nutty taste—this isn't your usual barbecue sauce. It also works well as a marinade for tofu, seitan, or mushrooms, and as a basting sauce.

MAKES 1¼ CUPS (310 ML)
Preparation time: *10 minutes*

3 tbsp tomato paste
2 tbsp smooth natural peanut butter
2 tbsp agave (see p. 250)
2 tbsp lime juice
1 tbsp adobo sauce
½ tsp liquid smoke
½ tsp ground cumin
½ tsp onion powder
½ tsp garlic powder
salt and ground black pepper, to taste

In a small bowl, whisk together tomato paste, peanut butter, agave, lime juice, adobo sauce, ¼ cup (60 mL) water, liquid smoke, cumin, onion powder, and garlic powder until combined well and smooth.

Add more water if needed. Taste and season as desired.

This recipe uses only the sauce from a can of chipotles in adobo, but if you want more heat, you can mince a chipotle and add it.

Smoky Barbecue Sauce

I find commercial barbecue sauces too sweet, so I like to make my own and use it as a basting or dipping sauce or marinade. This one is smoky and a little tart—feel free to increase the maple syrup if you find it too tart. Perfect with tofu, tempeh, or mushrooms at your next barbecue feast.

MAKES ¾ CUP (185 ML)
Preparation time: 5 minutes
Cooking time: 5 minutes

2½ tbsp tomato paste
2 tbsp maple syrup
2 tbsp lime juice
2 tbsp rice wine vinegar
1 tbsp balsamic or red wine vinegar
2 tbsp soy sauce
1½ tsp blackstrap molasses
1½ tsp liquid smoke
salt, ground black pepper, and hot sauce, to taste

For basting or dipping sauce
In a small saucepan on medium heat, whisk together tomato paste, syrup, lime juice, vinegars, soy sauce, molasses, and liquid smoke. Cook for 5 minutes, but do not let it boil. Taste and season as desired.

For marinade
In a large flat container with a resealable lid, whisk together all ingredients. Taste and season as desired.

Cilantro Barbecue Sauce

Sweet and tangy with a touch of spice, this barbecue sauce adds the flavor of cilantro to your meal. Use as a marinade, basting sauce, or dipping sauce for grilled vegetables. If you love cilantro, this one's for you!

MAKES 1 CUP (250 ML)
Preparation time: *10 minutes*

2 cups (500 mL) loosely packed cilantro
¼ cup (60 mL) ketchup
¼ cup (60 mL) lime juice
2 tbsp canola oil
3 tbsp tomato paste
1 tbsp hot sauce
1 tsp ground coriander
salt and ground black pepper, to taste

In a blender or food processor, pulse cilantro to a paste. Add ketchup, lime juice, oil, tomato paste, hot sauce, and coriander. Pulse to combine.

Add ¾–1 cup (185–250 mL) water, ¼ cup (60 mL) at a time, blending after each addition, until desired thickness is reached. Taste and season as desired.

Melon & Corn Salsa

I really like a summer salsa made from fruit; it's refreshing and sweet and goes with pretty much anything. I recommend using this as a topping for Pumpkin & Corn Cakes (p. 32).

MAKES 2 CUPS (500 ML)
Preparation time: 10 minutes + 1 hour chilling

2 tbsp finely chopped fresh mint

1 tbsp fresh lime juice

1 tbsp white balsamic vinegar (see p. 252)

1 tsp agave (see p. 250)

½–1 jalapeño, minced (optional)

1 cup (250 mL) finely chopped seeded cantaloupe

1 cup (250 mL) finely chopped seeded honeydew melon

¾ cup (1 cob) fresh corn kernels, or thawed frozen, or drained and rinsed canned corn

salt and ground black pepper, to taste

In a large bowl, whisk together mint, lime juice, vinegar, agave, and jalapeño. Add cantaloupe, melon, and corn, and toss gently to combine.

Chill for at least 1 hour, then toss again before serving. Taste, season, and adjust acid and sweetness as desired.

Fresh Tomato & Pepper Salsa

I love this with Slow Cooker Tomatillo & Tomato Tamales (p. 43), alongside just about anything cooked on the barbecue, as a topping for nachos, or as a dip with crackers. A touch of olive oil is lovely, but it is also good without.

MAKES 1½ CUPS (375 ML)
Preparation time: *15 minutes + 1 hour chilling*

3–4 medium Roma tomatoes, halved, seeded, and finely chopped

¼ cup (60 mL) finely chopped red bell peppers

¼ cup (60 mL) finely chopped yellow bell peppers

1 jalapeño, minced

1 garlic clove, minced

¼ cup (60 mL) finely chopped spring onions, about 3 onions

2 tbsp finely chopped cilantro

1 tbsp fresh lime juice

1 tbsp olive oil (optional)

salt and ground black pepper, to taste

In a large bowl, combine tomatoes, peppers, jalapeño, garlic, onions, cilantro, and lime juice. Mix to combine well. Stir in oil.

Chill for 1 hour, then bring back to room temperature before serving. Taste and season as desired.

Cucumber & Kiwifruit Salsa

"Refreshing" is the word that immediately springs to mind for this salsa, which is a little sweet, a little sour, cooling, and tasty. Make sure the kiwifruit are fully ripe; they should give if squeezed gently and have a sweet aroma. Enjoy this on grilled tofu, with Cider-Battered Tofu (p. 49), or anything else deep-fried!

MAKES 2 CUPS (500 mL)
Preparation time: 10 minutes + 1 hour chilling

1 tbsp fresh lime juice
½–1 jalapeño, finely chopped
1 small shallot, finely chopped
½ tsp grated fresh ginger
½ tsp lime zest
¼ tsp salt
1 cup (250 mL) finely chopped, peeled, ripe kiwifruit, about 2 large
1 cup (250 mL) finely chopped, seeded, but not peeled cucumber
1 tbsp finely chopped fresh mint
salt and ground black pepper, to taste

In a large bowl, combine juice, jalapeño, shallots, ginger, lime zest, and salt. Add kiwifruit, cucumber, and mint and toss to combine.

Chill for 1 hour before serving. Taste and season as desired.

As a New Zealander, I refuse to refer to the fruit with anything less than its full name. To me, a Kiwi is our native bird, an endangered species!

Peach Salsa

Specifically created to accompany Seitan Skewers with Peach Salsa (p. 170), this recipe is good on anything you'd like to barbecue. It also makes an appealing addition to Vanilla (p. 206) or Coconut (p. 210) Ice Cream. Try to use freestone peaches; they're so much easier to work with. To peel, quarter the peaches, remove the stone, and use a sharp knife to remove the very thin layer of skin.

MAKES 2¼ CUPS (560 ML).

Preparation time: *20 minutes + 1 hour chilling*

2 cups (500 mL) finely chopped, peeled peaches (2 or 3 large)
¼ cup (60 mL) finely chopped red bell peppers
¼ cup (60 mL) finely chopped red onions
2 tbsp lime juice
2 tbsp finely chopped cilantro
1 garlic clove, minced
1 tsp grated fresh ginger
½–1 jalapeño, seeded and cored, minced, to taste

In a small bowl, combine all ingredients and toss to mix well. Cover and refrigerate for at least 1 hour before serving.

Artichoke & Sunflower Seed Pesto

Pestos are usually made with pine nuts, but they can be expensive; sunflower seeds, less so. Once toasted, the sunflower seeds give a wonderful nuttiness so you won't miss the pine nuts. Artichoke hearts add a certain "cheesiness" to the pesto. I love this on vegetables or as a sandwich spread.

MAKES 1½ CUPS (375 ML)
Preparation time: *10 minutes*

1 cup (250 mL) toasted sunflower seeds

2 cups (500 mL) loosely packed fresh basil leaves

1 cup (250 mL) roughly chopped canned artichoke hearts, drained and rinsed

4 garlic cloves, roughly chopped

⅓ cup (80 mL) nutritional yeast (see p. 251)

¼ cup (60 mL) olive oil

1 tbsp lemon juice

salt and ground black pepper, to taste

In a food processor or blender, pulse sunflower seeds until very smooth. Add basil, artichokes, garlic, nutritional yeast, oil, and lemon juice and blend until smooth. Stop to scrape sides of bowl down as required.

Taste and season as desired.

Corn Relish

This relish is thick without being overly so, sweet, and a little spicy-sour. It's a great topping for a grilled veggie dog, veggie burger, or alongside some grilled tofu smothered in Smoky Barbecue Sauce (p. 73).

MAKES 1½ CUPS (375 ML)
Preparation time: *10 minutes*
Cooking time: *55 minutes*

1 tbsp olive oil

2 garlic cloves, minced

1 medium onion, finely chopped

1 Serrano pepper, minced

½ cup (125 mL) finely chopped red bell peppers

1½ cups (375 mL) corn kernels, about 2 cobs (reserve liquid if using fresh corn)

1 tsp salt

½ tsp ground black pepper

1½ tbsp white balsamic vinegar (see p. 252)

2 tsp arrowroot powder (see p. 250)

In a large saucepan on medium-high, heat oil. Sauté garlic, onions, and peppers for 6 minutes, until they start to caramelize. Stir in corn kernels, 1½ cups (375 mL) water, salt, pepper, and vinegar. Reduce heat to medium-low and cook, uncovered, stirring occasionally for about 45 minutes until reduced and thick. Turn off heat but leave on element.

In a small bowl, mix arrowroot with 2 tbsp water to create a slurry. Stir into warm corn mixture to thicken. Once thickened, remove from element and cool to room temperature.

Store in covered containers in refrigerator.

Chili & Tomato Jam

Sweet and slightly spiced, this savory jam (or relish) will elevate the humble veggie dog or burger at your next cookout to gourmet status! It's delicious spread on sandwich bread and definitely adds a little more oomph to the filling.

MAKES 2½ CUPS (625 mL)
Preparation time: 15 minutes
Cooking time: 2½ hours

1 tbsp olive oil

2 lb (1 kg) Roma tomatoes, seeded and roughly chopped, about 12

2 red bell peppers, seeded and roughly chopped

1 habañero, scored to taste (see note, below)

1 tsp sugar

½ tsp salt

¼ tsp ground black pepper

½ cup (125 mL) peeled, cored, and grated sweet apple, such as Gala, ½ medium

In a large saucepan on medium high, heat oil. Add tomatoes and sauté for 2 minutes, until juices start to run out. Stir in bell peppers, habañero, sugar, salt, and pepper. Reduce heat to medium-low and cook, uncovered, stirring occasionally, for 1 hour, until thick.

Stir in apple and 1 cup (250 mL) water. Cook, uncovered, for a further 1½ hours, until very thick but still chunky. Cool to room temperature. Remove habañero.

Store in covered containers in refrigerator.

Score the habañero to allow its flavor and a little of its spiciness to seep into the jam as it cooks. For more heat, make additional scores. If you don't want too much heat, start with 1 cut.

Jalapeño & Cherry Jam

It's a relish, but calling it "jam" seems to be the thing! This spicy-sweet combination is lovely served on veggie burgers, hot dogs, grilled tofu, or even as a spicy smear on crackers or savory scones. I think you'll love the combination. If you make a double batch (when the cherry tree is loaded with fruit), this is a beautiful dinner party gift when presented in a nice jar tied with a pretty ribbon.

MAKES 1 CUP (250 ML)
Preparation time: *20 minutes*
Cooking time: *45 minutes*

1 tbsp olive oil

1 tsp whole cumin seeds

1 garlic clove, minced

1 onion, finely chopped

3 jalapeños, seeded and minced

2 cups (500 mL) pitted, roughly chopped, sweet cherries, about 1 lb (500 g) whole cherries

½ cup (125 mL) peeled, cored, and grated sweet apple, such as Gala, about ½ medium

1 tsp sugar

½ tsp salt

¼ tsp ground black pepper

1 tsp white balsamic vinegar (see p. 252)

In a large saucepan on medium-high, heat oil. Add cumin seeds, allow to sizzle, then add garlic and onions and sauté for 5 minutes until soft and lightly browned. Stir in jalapeños, cherries, apple, sugar, salt, and pepper. Reduce heat to medium-low and cook, uncovered, stirring occasionally, for 40–50 minutes, until very thick. Stir more at beginning of cooking time, until fruit has released its juices.

Remove from heat and stir in vinegar. Cool completely, up to 1 hour.

Store in airtight covered containers in refrigerator.

Massaged Red Onions & Cumin

This condiment brings a zing of brightness and zap of crunch to a taco, burrito, or wrap, the Grilled Eggplant Sandwich (p. 101), Aussie Falafel (p. 102), or even a mixed salad. Try sprinkling it over perfectly ripe tomato slices.

MAKES 4–6 SERVINGS
Preparation time: 10 minutes + 1 hour chilling

1 red onion, halved and very thinly sliced
2 garlic cloves, very finely minced
½ tsp salt
½ tsp whole cumin seeds
¼ tsp ground cumin
2 tbsp lime juice
¼ cup (60 mL) white balsamic vinegar (see p. 252)

In a ziplock plastic bag, combine all ingredients.

Remove excess air and seal bag. Massage ingredients for 2 minutes to combine well.

Refrigerate for at least 1 hour before serving.

Use either roasted garlic or the Stovetop Poached Garlic (p. 21) for a mellower flavor.

Don't Hold the Mayo!

A standard in practically every fridge, this condiment is one from which you can create an almost unlimited number of variations and adaptations, depending on your inclination and imagination. Mayo, in the vegan forms of Tofonnaise (p. 110) or Nutonnaise (p. 111), is the base for the following recipes.

Aioli

Use Stovetop Poached Garlic Oil (p. 21) instead of grapeseed and olive oils and add 3 Stovetop Poached Garlic cloves (or to taste) to original recipe.

Tartar Sauce

Finely chop 2 tbsp capers, ¼ cup (60 mL) pickles (your choice), and 1 tbsp fresh parsley and add, along with 1 tbsp pickle juice (or to taste), to original recipe.

Agave Mustard Mayo

Add additional 1 tbsp agave (see p. 250) and 1 tbsp prepared grainy mustard to original recipe.

Chipotle Mayo

In a blender, process 1 seeded chipotle in adobo (see p. 250) until smooth. Stir into original recipe. Add more chipotle if you like things spicier.

Peppercorn & Lemon Mayo

Add 1 tbsp cracked peppercorns and ½ tsp lemon zest with a dash of lemon juice to original recipe.

I'M SHARING SOME OF MY SANDWICH *favorites, including spreads to use in building your own, as well as hints on the perfect mix-and-match sandwich combinations. Prepare sandwiches in advance to take on a picnic by wrapping them individually in parchment paper, or store the ingredients separately in plastic containers (the sandwich deconstructed, if you will) and put it all together when you arrive at your destination.*

sandwiches & spreads

Sandwiches made simple

From the fanciest to the simplest, there's nothing quite like a sandwich!

Breads

With such a wide range of breads to choose from—from home-made to store-bought, from thinly sliced to baguettes and buns—start by simply choosing a bread you like, then mix and match until you find a combination of bread and filling(s) that works for you.

I like very thinly sliced plain sandwich bread for simple tea (or finger) sandwiches. Heavy pumpernickel works well for open sandwiches, and pitas are great for stuffing. I prefer crustier, heartier bread if loading sandwiches with spreads and vegetables.

When purchasing bread, carefully read labels to look for and avoid animal ingredients or additives such as honey, milk powder, whey, and egg wash.

Fillings

Pretty much anything can be used to fill a sandwich, so be creative and combine flavors you like. Use a condiment such as the Red Bell Pepper & Sun-dried Tomato Spread (p. 90) combined with the best quality produce you can buy—lettuce, tomatoes, sprouts, cucumbers, avocados, and whatever else takes your fancy—with or without vegan mayo (plain or flavored), but don't limit yourself to raw vegetables. Roasted veggies, such as in the Grilled Eggplant Sandwich (p. 101), are delicious on chewy or hearty bread.

Tea or finger sandwiches are simple and delicate, usually crustless, and generally have just one filling, with a flavored vegan butter or mayonnaise spread. Recipes for these sandwiches include my quartet of "inspired" sandwich fillings (pp. 93–99) or single produce items such as watercress, sprouts, cucumber, cooked asparagus, tomatoes, or thinly sliced commercial or home-made vegan cold cuts or cheeses.

Construction Tips

Once you've chosen your bread and fillings, all you need to do is put it all together.

For fancy sandwiches, use the thinnest sliced bread you can find, keep the fillings simple (as mentioned above), and cut the crusts off. As the bread is likely to dry out more quickly once crusts are removed, cover sandwiches with cling film and refrigerate if making them in advance. Spread the bread with flavored (or plain) vegan butter (or mayonnaise), add a single layer of filling, then remove crusts before slicing into desired shape—squares, rectangles, or triangles. These should be bite-sized sandwiches.

For open-faced sandwiches, use a firmer bread that won't get soggy or break—and don't overload them, or the fillings will fall right off.

Flavored Vegan Margarine

Something as simple as a flavored margarine spread onto fresh bread, with perfectly ripe tomatoes, makes the most delicious sandwiches!

2–3 tbsp any ingredients below, in any combination or alone, to taste
½ cup (125 mL) vegan margarine
salt and ground black pepper, to taste

Add flavorings as desired to vegan margarine, season to taste, and mix very well. This method also works for flavoring mayonnaise.

- finely chopped arugula
- blended artichoke hearts
- blended roasted red bell peppers
- mashed capers
- mashed caramelized onions
- minced chipotle in adobo (see p. 250)
- chives and mashed Stovetop Poached Garlic (p. 21)
- smooth or grainy Dijon mustard
- chopped fresh corn
- grated shallots
- cooked and blended green peas
- grated horseradish
- minced Kalamata olives
- lemon zest and minced fresh parsley
- lime zest and minced cilantro
- miso paste (see p. 251)
- minced fresh herbs such as thyme, mint, lavender
- peanut (or other nut) butter
- pesto
- minced sun-dried tomatoes

Red Bell Pepper & Sun-dried Tomato Spread

This spread reminds me of the creamy sour cream and packet soup mixes I used to make as a child—it's a tomato variation. I think it's perfect for any sandwich, but especially nice if paired with fresh-from-the-garden, sun-ripened tomatoes and crisp lettuce.

MAKES 1 CUP (250 ML)
Preparation time: 10 minutes + 1 hour chilling

½ cup (125 mL) soft regular (water-packed) or silken tofu

⅓ cup (80 mL) vegan cream cheese

2 tbsp finely chopped red bell peppers

1 tbsp finely chopped sun-dried tomatoes

1 shallot, finely chopped

1 garlic clove, minced

1 tbsp vegan mayonnaise such as Tofonnaise (p. 110)

1 tbsp lemon juice

½ tsp tomato paste

salt and ground black pepper, to taste

In a blender or food processor, pulse together tofu, cream cheese, red bell peppers, sun-dried tomatoes, shallots, garlic, mayonnaise, lemon juice, and tomato paste until combined well. Taste and season as desired. Chill for at least 1 hour before using.

Coronation Tofu

There's a little history in this recipe. The original was a chicken dish initially created for the banquet to celebrate the coronation of Queen Elizabeth II in 1953. My version uses tofu, but otherwise is quite similar. This is traditionally eaten as a salad or used as a sandwich filling.

MAKES 4 SERVINGS

Preparation time: 10 minutes + 1 hour chilling

Cooking time: 25 minutes

1 lb (500 g) extra-firm regular tofu (water-packed), diced

1 tbsp grapeseed oil

½ cup (125 mL) finely chopped onion, about ½ medium

½ cup (125 mL) red wine

3 tbsp lemon juice

1 tbsp tomato paste

1 tbsp curry powder

1 tbsp agave (see p. 250)

1 bay leaf

⅓ cup (80 mL) finely chopped dried apricots, about 6

½ cup (125 mL) vegan mayonnaise such as Tofonnaise (p. 110)

⅓ cup (80 mL) plain vegan yogurt

In a large non-stick frying pan on medium heat, dry sauté tofu for 8 minutes, stirring occasionally, until all sides are lightly browned. Transfer to serving bowl and set aside.

Heat oil in same pan on medium. Sauté onions for 5 minutes, until soft. Stir in wine, lemon juice, tomato paste, curry powder, and agave and mix to combine well. Add bay leaf and apricots and cook, uncovered, for 7–9 minutes, until liquid is absorbed and mixture is reduced and thick.

Remove from heat and stir in mayonnaise, yogurt, and tofu. Transfer to serving bowl and chill for at least 1 hour.

Remove bay leaf before serving.

Egg Salad-Inspired Sandwich Filling

One of my testers suggested using Creamy Coleslaw Dressing (p. 113) as a base for an egg-less salad, and it was a great suggestion! If you're making this on a hot day and can't face the stove, you can skip the step of dry sautéing the tofu and still get a good result.

MAKES 2 CUPS (500 ML)

Preparation time: 15 minutes + 1 hour chilling

8 oz (230 g) firm regular tofu (water-packed), finely diced

¼ cup (60 mL) Creamy Coleslaw Dressing (p. 113)

¼ tsp ground turmeric

¼ tsp ground cumin

⅛ tsp black salt (see p. 250)

2 tbsp finely chopped celery

2 tbsp finely chopped spring onions, 1 medium

salt and ground black pepper, to taste

In a large non-stick frying pan on medium heat, dry-sauté tofu for 5–7 minutes, until golden, turning as required. Remove from pan, transfer to a large bowl, and roughly mash to break into small irregular pieces.

Stir in dressing, turmeric, cumin, black salt, celery, and spring onions, and mix to combine well. Taste and season as desired.

Chill for 1 hour before using.

Tuna Salad-Inspired Sandwich Filling

Jackfruit is a surprisingly wonderful replacement for tuna in this cruelty-free sandwich filling. It remains quite briny even after rinsing, and when cooked becomes very tuna-like in appearance. Note: buy canned young jackfruit in brine, not mature jackfruit in syrup for this recipe.

MAKES 2 CUPS (500 ML)

Preparation time: *30 minutes + 1 hour chilling*

 *or* **n** *(in mayonnaise)*

1 tbsp olive oil

2 garlic cloves, minced

½ medium onion, finely chopped

2 cups (500 mL) canned jackfruit in brine, drained and rinsed or 19-oz (540-mL) can (see p. 251)

¼ cup (60 mL) vegan mayonnaise such as Tofonnaise (p. 110)

1 tsp prepared smooth Dijon mustard

1 tsp dried dill

¼ cup (60 mL) packed, finely shredded toasted nori (see p. 251)

1 celery stalk, finely chopped

¼ cup (60 mL) finely chopped dill pickle (spicy, if desired)

salt and ground black pepper, to taste

In a large frying pan on medium, heat oil. Sauté garlic and onions for 5 minutes, until soft. Add jackfruit and sauté for 10 minutes, until lightly caramelized and easily broken up into small stringy pieces. Remove from heat, roughly mash to break up jackfruit, then cool for 20 minutes, or to room temperature.

In a large bowl, whisk together mayonnaise and mustard. Stir in dill, nori, celery, and pickles.

Stir in jackfruit. Taste and season as desired.

Chill for at least 1 hour before using.

Roll nori sheet into a cylinder, then slice thinly for easiest shredding, or crumble in a spice grinder.

Crab Salad-Inspired Sandwich Filling

I'm told that crab has a smooth mouth-feel, which is why I use creamy, cooked lima beans as the base for this sandwich filling. I'm not sure if this is anything like crab salad, but it sure tastes good!

MAKES 2 CUPS (500 ML)

Preparation time: 30 minutes + 1 hour chilling

 or *(in mayonnaise)*

1½ cups (375 mL) cooked lima beans, or 14-oz (398-mL) can, drained and rinsed

½ cup (125 mL) corn kernels (fresh or frozen and thawed)

¼ cup (60 mL) finely chopped green bell peppers

¼ cup (60 mL) finely chopped spring onions

¼ cup (60 mL) vegan mayonnaise such as Tofonnaise (p. 110)

2 tbsp green relish

1 tsp lemon juice

½ tsp dried dill

salt and ground black pepper, to taste

In a large bowl, mash lima beans with a fork until chunky but all broken up. Mix in corn, green bell peppers, onions, mayonnaise, relish, lemon juice, and dill. Taste and season as desired.

Chill for at least 1 hour before using.

Use cream-colored, dried (and cooked) or canned lima beans, not green, fresh, or frozen.

Chicken Salad-Inspired Sandwich Filling

The tempeh, which stands in for chicken, is seasoned as I would expect chicken salad to be in this recipe—and isn't most of the flavor really contained in the seasonings? The result here is moist and tasty, perfect for picnic sandwiches.

MAKES 2 CUPS (500 ML)
Preparation time: 30 minutes + 1 hour chilling

2 tsp apple cider vinegar

8 oz (230 g) tempeh (whole pieces) (see p. 252)

1 tbsp olive oil

½ tsp sesame oil

1 tsp Faux Poultry Seasoning Mix (p. 19)

¼ cup (60 mL) vegan mayonnaise such as Tofonnaise (p. 110)

2 cloves Stovetop Poached Garlic (p. 21), finely chopped

½ tsp prepared smooth Dijon mustard

2 tbsp finely chopped red bell peppers

2 tbsp finely chopped green bell peppers

½ jalapeño, minced, or to taste

salt and ground black pepper, to taste

In a medium frying pan on high, bring vinegar and 2 cups (500 mL) water to a boil. Add tempeh, reduce heat to medium, cover, and cook for 5 minutes. Turn and cook for another 5 minutes. Remove from heat, discard cooking water, and refresh tempeh under cold water until cool to the touch.

Cut tempeh into ½-in (1-cm) cubes and place in a bowl. Add oils and poultry seasoning to tempeh and rub to coat.

In a large non-stick frying pan on medium-high heat, sauté tempeh for 5 minutes, stirring, until golden on all sides. Return tempeh to bowl and roughly mash with a fork to break up. Cool for 10 minutes, to room temperature.

Stir in mayonnaise, garlic, mustard, bell peppers, and jalapeño, and mix to combine well. Taste and season as desired.

Chill for 1 hour before using.

Grilled Eggplant Sandwiches

Simple yet full of wonderful texture and flavor, these sandwiches can be prepared ahead of time and taken with you if there are no cooking facilities at your picnic spot. However, if you can grill on location, bring the marinated eggplant in containers and put sandwiches together using eggplant strips hot off the grill (I would recommend this second option!).

MAKES 4 SERVINGS
Preparation time: 15 minutes + 1 hour marinating
Cooking time: 20 minutes

 (bread only)

 (in margarine)

1 medium eggplant, about 1 lb (500 g)

MARINADE
2 tbsp olive oil
2 garlic cloves, minced
¼ cup (60 mL) white wine or vegetable stock
2 tbsp white balsamic vinegar (see p. 252)
2 tsp toasted cumin seeds
1 tsp smoked paprika
½ tsp dried tarragon
¼–½ tsp chili flakes
salt and ground black pepper, to taste

CHIVE BUTTER
¼ cup (60 mL) finely chopped fresh chives
2 tbsp finely chopped shallots
½ cup (125 mL) vegan margarine

TO ASSEMBLE
4 long baguette-style rolls
2 fresh ripe tomatoes, sliced
2 cups baby arugula, baby spinach, or lettuce leaves
Massaged Red Onions & Cumin (p. 84) (optional)

In a large flat container with a resealable lid or in a large ziplock bag, combine all marinade ingredients.

Cut eggplant in half lengthwise, then into 16 ¼-in (6-mm) wide strips. Place eggplant slices in bag with marinade and toss to coat. Marinate for at least 1 hour (longer is better). Turn after 30 minutes.

In a small bowl, combine chive butter ingredients. Cover and chill until required.

Preheat barbecue to high (or broiler, if using oven) and grill eggplant slices for 20 minutes, turning as required until both sides are golden and a little caramelized. While grilling, split rolls lengthwise and lightly toast if desired.

Spread rolls with chive butter. Place tomato slices, greens, and red onions on 1 side of each sandwich. Top each with 4 slices of grilled eggplant.

Massaged Red Onions & Cumin adds another dimension of flavor to this sandwich.

Aussie Falafel

When I lived in Port Douglas in Far North Queensland, Australia, I used to drive down to Cairns on my days off and quite often found myself some yummy falafel to eat. This is a re-creation of that taste sensation, but made mini! Note: Dried chickpeas need to be soaked for at least 24 hours beforehand.

MAKES 6–8 SERVINGS

Preparation time: *30 minutes + 1 hour chilling*
Cooking time: *10 minutes*
Sandwich assembly time: *10 minutes*

  (bread only)

FALAFEL

½ cup (125 mL) dried chickpeas, soaked in water to cover for 24 hours, drained, and rinsed
¾ cup (185 mL) cooked chickpeas (if canned, drain and rinse)
3 heaping tbsp fresh parsley
1 shallot, roughly chopped
2 garlic cloves, roughly chopped
1 tbsp tahini (see p. 252)
1½ tsp ground flaxseeds
1½ tsp lemon juice
1½ tsp soy sauce
1 tsp ground cumin
½ tsp salt
½ tsp smoked paprika
¼ tsp dried marjoram
¼ tsp ground coriander
¼ tsp ground black pepper
⅛ tsp ground turmeric
⅛–½ tsp chili flakes, to taste (optional)
¾ cup (185 mL) + 2½ tbsp chickpea flour (see p. 251)
2 tbsp olive oil

BREAD

7 whole wheat pita pockets

FILLINGS

½ cup (125 mL) hummus, such as Tandoori Spiced Hummus (p. 67)
½ cup (125 mL) salad vegetables per ½ pita, including but not limited to sliced tomatoes, lettuce leaves, alfalfa sprouts, sliced cucumbers, sliced red onions
1–2 tbsp condiments per ½ pita, such as Massaged Red Onions & Cumin (p. 84) or Cucumber & Kiwifruit Salsa (p. 77)

1 recipe Quick Tahini Falafel Sauce (p. 56)

Make falafel

In a food processor or powerful blender, pulse soaked chickpeas until completely smooth and paste-like. Stop to scrape down sides of bowl as required.

Add cooked chickpeas, parsley, shallots, and garlic and pulse until combined well. Add tahini, flax-seeds, lemon juice, soy sauce, cumin, salt, paprika, marjoram, coriander, pepper, turmeric, and chili flakes and pulse until smooth.

Add chickpea flour and pulse to just combine. The mix will resemble cookie dough and should hold together easily if pressed. Place food processor bowl in refrigerator and chill for at least 1 hour.

Line a baking sheet or large plate with parchment paper. Scoop heaped 1-tbsp portions of mixture and, with dampened hands, shape into 2-in (5-cm) diameter patties. Place patties on baking sheet.

In a large non-stick frying pan on medium, heat a very thin layer of oil. Fry patties 6 at a time for 2–3 minutes per side, until golden brown. Place cooked patties on parchment-lined sheet to absorb excess oil.

Assemble sandwiches

Preheat oven to 350°F (180°C).

Heat each pita in turn so it becomes soft and pliable.

Cut each pita in half and gently open pocket. Spread a layer of hummus or Quick Tahini Falafel Sauce inside each pocket. Layer salad vegetables on top of hummus.

Tuck three falafel patties into pocket. Drizzle with a generous amount of Quick Tahini Falafel Sauce.

These are also wonderful served over rice and grilled vegetables, as a finger food starter on mini-pita bread cut-outs (use a cookie cutter and cut rounds from pita bread or whole wheat tortilla) with a slice of tomato and a drizzle of Quick Tahini Falafel Sauce, which is easy to use from a plastic squeeze bottle.

If serving these at a picnic, I bring the cooked falafel, salad, sauce, and pita in separate containers and assemble once there. You can wrap pita in foil and place on barbecue away from direct heat for a few minutes to soften before filling.

Pita Po' Boys

Some people believe that Po' Boys are all about the bread, while others are convinced they're all about the sauce. Either way, no one is going to mistake this for the "real" thing, but it sure tastes good! I use a spicy mayonnaise-based condiment incorporating that wonderful Louisiana product, Tabasco sauce. Don't use the delicious Po' Boy Mayo just for these sandwiches—it's good served with Cider-Battered Tofu (p. 49), as a dip for Spiced Oven Potato Wedges (p. 174), or even with crudités.

MAKES 4 SANDWICHES OR 2–4 SERVINGS

Preparation time: *15 minutes, not including time to make Twice-Fried Seitan Bites*

PO' BOY MAYO

½ cup (125 mL) vegan mayonnaise such as Tofonnaise (p. 110)

2 garlic cloves, minced

¼ cup (60 mL) minced bread-and-butter pickles

½ tsp (or to taste) Tabasco or other hot sauce

½ tsp paprika

1 tsp onion powder

2 tsp lemon juice

SANDWICH

2 pita pockets

4 lettuce leaves

½ cup (125 mL) shredded cabbage or bagged coleslaw mix

24 Twice-Fried Seitan Bites (p. 36)— 6 per ½ pita

In a medium bowl, combine all Po'Boy Mayo ingredients until mixed well. Cover and chill if not using immediately.

Preheat oven to 250°F (120°C). Heat pita pockets for 5 minutes, until soft and pliable. Remove from oven.

Cut each pita in half and gently open pocket. Spread a generous layer of Po' Boy Mayo inside each pocket.

Line each pita half with a lettuce leaf and top with equal amounts of cabbage. Place 6 Seitan Bites in each pocket and top with any remaining Po' Boy Mayo.

For a more authentic Po' Boy experience, use the freshest, crustiest, chewiest French bread baguette you can find instead of pita.

Meat-y Ball Sandwich

Hearty street food, anyone? These sandwiches are super filling and so very good—great for those coming off a game of touch football in the backyard. The non-meat balls are made from scratch—if you prepare these in advance, reheat them before assembling the sandwiches. (Tip: Serve these Meat-y Balls over pasta; double the quantities given for making the sauce.)

MAKES 6 SERVINGS

Preparation time: *25 minutes, divided*
Cooking time: *25 minutes*

6 submarine sandwich-size rolls, or baguettes, halved

MEAT-Y BALLS

1 tbsp tomato paste
1 tsp soy sauce
¾ cup (185 mL) TVP granules (see p. 252)
1 cup (250 mL) cooked cannellini (white kidney) beans (if canned, drain and rinse)
2 tbsp olive oil
½ tsp dried oregano
½ tsp dried marjoram
½ tsp dried basil
½ tsp garlic powder
½ tsp onion powder
½ tsp salt
⅛ tsp ground black pepper
⅛ tsp ground fennel seeds
⅛ tsp chili flakes
1½ cups (375 mL) vital wheat gluten powder (see p. 252)

SAUCE

3 cups (750 mL) tomato juice, room temperature
1½ cups (375 mL) vegetable stock
1½ tsp balsamic vinegar
1 tsp garlic powder
1 tsp onion powder
1 tsp dried basil

1 tbsp olive oil
1½ cups (625 mL) shredded vegan cheese, to garnish

Prepare rolls

Slice rolls lengthwise, spread both cut surfaces with Basil Butter (see right-hand column), close, and place in refrigerator until required.

Make Meat-y Balls and Sauce

In a large bowl, combine ¾ cup (185 mL) + 2 tbsp boiling water, tomato paste, and soy sauce. Add TVP granules, cover, and let sit for 10 minutes to reconstitute.

In a food processor, blend beans, oil, oregano, marjoram, basil, garlic powder, onion powder, salt, pepper, fennel seeds, and chili flakes until smooth. Stop to scrape down sides of bowl as required. Stir into TVP mix and combine well.

Stir in gluten powder and mix well. Knead in bowl with your hands for 2 or 3 minutes to activate gluten and incorporate the TVP. If TVP doesn't adhere to dough, keep kneading and shaping.

Shape mixture into 36 1-tbsp-sized balls and let rest for 5 minutes.

In a small bowl, prepare sauce: mix together tomato juice, vegetable stock, balsamic vinegar, garlic powder, onion powder, and basil.

In a large frying pan on medium-high, heat 1 tbsp olive oil. Sear TVP balls in batches—do not overcrowd the pan—for 5–7 minutes, turning as required, to seal, partially cook, and brown, forming a crust.

Add sauce to pan. Cook for 15 minutes, until balls have expanded a little, are firm yet moist, and cooked all the way through, and liquid is mostly absorbed and reduced.

Assemble sandwiches

Preheat broiler to high. Line a medium baking sheet with parchment paper. Open rolls and set, butter side up, on baking sheet. Broil until lightly toasted. Remove rolls but leave broiler on.

Place 6 balls on 1 side of each roll with some sauce. Cover balls with ¼ cup (60 mL) shredded vegan cheese and broil for 2 minutes, until melted. Close sandwiches and press down on tops for a moment before serving.

Basil Butter

½ cup (125 mL) vegan margarine
¼ cup (60 mL) finely chopped fresh basil
1 garlic clove, minced
¼ tsp onion powder
¼ tsp garlic powder

In a small bowl, combine all ingredients until mixed well.

USE THESE RECIPES TO
DRESS *any salad you choose,
whether mixed greens, hearty
kale, grain- or potato-based, or a
simple chopped vegetable salad.
If making a mixed green salad
for a picnic or cookout, take it
undressed. Keep the dressing in a
small container and add it later,
just before the salad is served, or
let everyone dress their own.*

salad
dressings

Tofonnaise

That would be Tofu-Mayonnaise, of course. It's not the same as a commercial vegan brand, but for a home-made, tofu-based mayo, it's pretty awesome—creamy, smooth, a little bit sweet, a little bit tart, and with nice overall balance. This is a good alternative for salads and sandwiches, and is the base for a whole heap of other salad dressings and a number of other recipes throughout this book. Straight out of the blender, its texture is reminiscent of yogurt, but it thickens after 1 hour or so in the refrigerator.

MAKES 2 CUPS (500 ML)
Preparation time: 5 minutes +
1 hour chilling

12 oz (340 g) silken tofu
2 tbsp lemon juice
2 tbsp grapeseed or canola oil
1 tbsp smooth Dijon or other mild
   mustard
1 tbsp white wine vinegar
1 tbsp olive oil
1 tbsp agave (see p. 250)
½ tsp onion powder
½ tsp salt

In a blender or food processor, process all ingredients together until smooth. Stop to scrape sides of bowl as required.

Transfer to a covered container and chill for at least 1 hour before using. Will keep in refrigerator for up to 1 week.

Nutonnaise

If you can't tolerate soy but want to make mayo-based dressings, here's one that's nut-based. It's quite thick and becomes more so after refrigeration; in this state, it's wonderful as a dip for crudités or as a topping for baked potatoes or barbecued corn on the cob. Note: You'll need to soak cashews overnight before preparing this recipe.

MAKES 2 CUPS (500 ML)
Preparation time: *10 minutes + soaking*

1½ cups (375 mL) raw cashews, soaked for 8 hours, drained and rinsed
¼ cup (60 mL) raw pine nuts
1 garlic clove, chopped
3 tbsp grapeseed oil
1 tbsp olive oil
2 tbsp lime juice
2 tbsp apple cider vinegar
1 tbsp white wine vinegar
1 tbsp smooth Dijon or other mild mustard
1 tbsp agave (see p. 250)
½ tsp onion powder
½ tsp salt

In a powerful blender or food processor, pulse cashews and pine nuts until broken up into pieces.

Add garlic, both oils, lime juice, both vinegars, mustard, agave, onion powder, and salt and pulse to combine. Add 6 tbsp water and blend until smooth. Stop to scrape sides of bowl as required. Add additional water as required.

Transfer to a covered container. Will keep in refrigerator for up to 1 week.

To get this super smooth, you'll need a high-powered blender. You can make this recipe without one, but the final results may be a little grainy.

1001 Island Dressing

Thousand Island is my husband's favorite salad dressing, and this vegan version exceeded his expectations of what a great dressing should be. It's tangy with hints of sweetness and adds a mouth-pleasing textural contrast to any salad.

MAKES 1½ CUPS (375 ML)

Preparation time: *5 minutes + 1 hour chilling*

 or *(in mayonnaise)*

1 cup (250 mL) vegan mayonnaise such as Tofonnaise (p. 110)

4 tbsp minced bread-and-butter pickles

2 tbsp tomato ketchup

1 tbsp minced red bell peppers

1 tbsp red wine vinegar

1 tsp minced capers

salt and ground black pepper, to taste

In a small bowl, mix mayonnaise, pickles, ketchup, peppers, vinegar, and capers until combined well. Taste and season as desired.

Chill for at least 1 hour before using. Will keep in refrigerator for up to 5 days.

Creamy Coleslaw Dressing

This is my new favorite-ever coleslaw dressing. Sometimes I simply stir it into 3–4 cups (750 mL–1 L) shredded cabbage for super simple, super tasty, almost instant coleslaw! I also like to use it as a base and jazz it up as in the recipes for Corn 'Slaw (p. 129) and Quinoa & Avocado 'Slaw (p. 131).

MAKES ½ CUP (125 ML)
Preparation time: *5 minutes*

 or *(in mayonnaise)*

¼ cup (60 mL) vegan mayonnaise such as Tofonnaise (p. 110)
1 tbsp smooth Dijon mustard
2 tbsp white balsamic vinegar (see p. 252)
2 tsp brown rice syrup (see p. 250)
1 tsp garlic powder
½ tsp ground dry mustard
½ tsp onion powder
½ tsp salt

In a large bowl (if using as a base for coleslaw), whisk together all ingredients. Whisk in about 1 tbsp water, 1 tsp at a time, until desired consistency is reached.

Use as directed in recipes, as noted above, or store in a covered container in refrigerator for up to 1 week.

Zingy Orange Mustard Dressing

This dressing will add a bright citrus-y note to your salad, tempered with a backdrop of smooth mustard. Great on hot or cold cooked greens. You can also mix it with shredded cabbage in a ziplock plastic bag and marinate for at least 1 hour for a tasty twist on 'slaw.

MAKES ½ CUP (125 ML)
Preparation time: 5 minutes

¼ cup (60 mL) freshly squeezed orange juice
2 tbsp smooth Dijon mustard
1 tbsp agave (see p. 250)
1 tbsp grapeseed oil
1 tsp orange zest
1 garlic clove, minced
salt and ground black pepper, to taste

In a small bowl, whisk together orange juice, mustard, agave, oil, orange zest, and garlic.

Taste and season as desired.

Raspberry Balsamic Dressing

I created this dressing one day when the raspberries I had in the refrigerator were a little past their prime, but it's best to use fresh ripe fruit. The taste is bright and a little sweet, but with nice undertones from the vinegar.

MAKES 1 CUP (250 ML)
Preparation time: 5 minutes + 1 hour chilling

½ cup (125 mL) very ripe fresh raspberries
2 tbsp grapeseed oil
1 tbsp white balsamic vinegar (see p. 252)
1 tbsp apple juice
1 garlic clove, chopped
2 tsp agave (see p. 250)
salt and ground black pepper, to taste

In a food processor or blender, blend raspberries, oil, vinegar, apple juice, garlic, and agave until smooth. Stop to scrape down sides of bowl as required.

Add 2 tbsp water, 1 tbsp at a time, until desired consistency is reached. Taste and season as desired. Strain through a fine sieve to remove seeds.

Chill for 1 hour.

Poached Garlic & White Wine Dressing

This slightly sweet but still tangy dressing is one of the many ways I like to use Stovetop Poached Garlic. Serve over a mixed green, arugula, or spinach salad with added nuts, seeds, and/or fruit. Best made and used on the same day. If you're making salad for a crowd, it doubles (and even triples) well.

MAKES ⅓ CUP (80 ML)
Preparation time: *5 minutes + time to make garlic recipes*

3 cloves Stovetop Poached Garlic (p. 21)

2 tbsp Garlic-Infused Oil (p. 21)

1 tbsp dry white wine (such as Sauvignon Blanc)

1 tbsp lemon juice

1 tbsp rice wine vinegar

1 tsp agave (see p. 250)

salt, to taste

In a small bowl, mash garlic to a paste. Whisk in oil until smooth.

Stir in wine, lemon juice, vinegar, agave and salt, and whisk until combined well.

Tangy Lemon Sour Cream Dressing

I hate it when there's just a little sour cream left in the bottom of the container; as there never seems to be enough to make anything from it—until now. This dressing, which requires just a touch of sour cream, tastes fresh and tart—and really good.

MAKES ⅓ CUP (80 mL)
Preparation time: *5 minutes*

¼ cup (60 mL) vegan sour cream such as Cheater Sour Cream (p. 23)
1 tbsp lemon juice
1 tsp lemon zest
1 tbsp smooth Dijon mustard
1 tsp agave (see p. 250)
1 drop liquid smoke
salt and ground black pepper, to taste.

In a small bowl, whisk sour cream, lemon juice and zest, mustard, agave, liquid smoke, and 1 tbsp water until smooth, creamy, and combined well. Taste and season as desired.

Use immediately or store in a covered container in refrigerator for up to 2 days.

Variation: stir in 1 tbsp of poppy seeds.

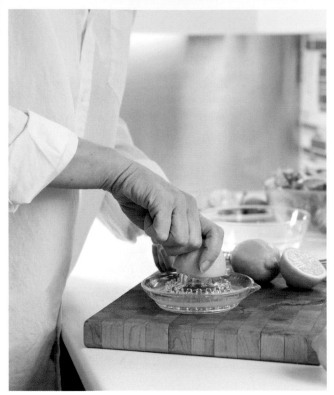

Sesame Lemon Dressing

I was inspired one day to make a thick and creamy dressing that was both soy-free and nut-free. It's big on both sesame and lemon flavors and thick enough to use as a dip.

MAKES 1½ CUPS (375 ML)
Preparation time: *10 minutes*

½ cup (125 mL) raw hulled sesame seeds
2 tbsp rice wine vinegar
2 tbsp lemon juice
1½ tbsp lemon zest
2 tbsp grapeseed oil
1 tbsp sesame oil
1 tbsp brown rice syrup (see p. 250)
1 garlic clove, minced
1 tsp grated fresh ginger
salt and ground black pepper, to taste

In a blender or food processor, blend sesame seeds, rice wine vinegar, lemon juice and zest, oils, syrup, garlic, and ginger until thick and smooth.

Add 5 tbsp water, 1 tbsp at a time, and blend until smooth. For a thinner dressing, add more water by the tbsp.

Taste and season as desired.

Garlicky Miso Dressing

A solid favorite of mine, this savory dressing has a little sharpness from the garlic, and complements a green salad really well. Try it over a simple spinach salad topped with berries and Savory Sunflower Brittle (p. 28). It's also good drizzled onto barbecued corn on the cob, used as a dressing for potato salad, or mixed into mashed potatoes.

MAKES ¾ CUP (185 mL)
Preparation time: *5 minutes + 1 hour chilling*

¼ cup (60 mL) silken tofu

2 tbsp rice wine vinegar

1 tbsp miso paste (see p. 251)

1 tbsp lemon juice

1 tbsp grapeseed oil

1 tbsp maple syrup

2 garlic cloves, chopped

½ tsp garlic powder

½ tsp soy sauce

salt and ground black pepper, to taste

In a food processor or blender, blend tofu, vinegar, miso, lemon juice, oil, syrup, garlic, garlic powder, and soy sauce until smooth. Stop to scrape down sides of bowl as required.

Add 2–3 tbsp water, 1 tbsp at a time, until desired consistency is reached. Taste and season as desired.

Chill for 1 hour. Will keep in a covered container in refrigerator for up to 5 days.

Fu'Tons

That's what I call my tofu croutons. They're a welcome addition to any salad, or anywhere you'd like an extra burst of tasty, crispy protein. I also use this as a topping for pasta dishes, but it's all up to you where and how to use these yummy herbed fu'tons. Tip: You can add any herbs or spices to the coating mix to complement the dish you're serving these with.

MAKES 4–6 SERVINGS AS A TOPPING
Preparation time: *10 minutes*
Cooking time: *10 minutes*

3 tbsp Garlic-Infused Oil (p. 21) or olive oil
½ cup (125 mL) white rice flour (see p. 251)
½ tsp garlic powder
½ tsp onion powder
¼ tsp dried thyme
¼ tsp dried oregano
¼ tsp salt
ground black pepper, to taste
1 lb (500 g) extra-firm regular tofu (water-packed), cubed to ½ in (1 cm)

Pour oil into a large shallow bowl and set aside.

In a different shallow bowl, combine rice flour, garlic powder, onion powder, thyme, oregano, salt, and pepper.

Toss tofu cubes in oil, then in flour mixture to coat well.

In a large non-stick frying pan on medium-high heat, sauté tofu cubes, stirring frequently, for 10 minutes, until all sides are golden and crispy.

Serve hot or cold.

Tofonnaise (p. 110)

Sesame Lemon Dressing (p. 119)

Fu'Tons (opposite)

Tangy Lemon Sour Cream Dressing (p. 117)

Raspberry Balsamic Dressing (p. 115)

Nutonnaise (p. 111)

THIS COLLECTION OF READY-TO-EAT *salads includes a huge range of variations on the theme, from those based on hearty grains to vegetable (raw or cooked) salads to those featuring potatoes and pasta, as well as variations on coleslaw. Use a large bowl with a resealable lid when taking ready-made salads to a picnic; you can also use it as a serving bowl. Many of these salads call for an hour of chilling time, which allows the flavors to completely meld. While recommended, this step can be omitted should you be short of time.*

ready built salads

Nutty Cauliflower Salad

In the summer, I'm always creating new ways to use cooked vegetables in salads. I prepare them in large quantities and then keep them in the refrigerator for a few days. I haven't specified the cooking method here, but you can make this recipe with cauliflower that's been lightly boiled, steamed, barbecued, or roasted. Each adds a slightly different flavor profile and texture to the salad.

MAKES 4–6 SERVINGS

Preparation time: 15 minutes, not including cooking and cooling cauliflower + 1 hour chilling

2 tbsp olive oil

1 tbsp grainy Dijon mustard

1 tbsp tahini (see p. 252)

1 tsp agave (see p. 250)

4 cups (1 L) cooked bite-sized cauliflower florets, about 1 medium head

¼ cup (60 mL) finely chopped spring onions

⅓ cup (80 mL) roasted and salted macadamia nuts, halved, or cashews

salt and ground black pepper, to taste

1 medium orange or mandarin orange, segmented

In a large bowl, whisk together oil, 2 tbsp water, mustard, tahini, and agave. Let sit for 10 minutes at room temperature to thicken slightly.

Stir in cauliflower, onions, and nuts and toss to coat. Taste and season as desired.

Gently toss orange segments into salad or arrange on top as garnish.

Chill for at least 1 hour before serving.

Green Bean Waldorf Salad

Green beans give a standard Waldorf another layer of flavor and texture, and capers add a pop of tartness, both of which complement the sweetness of the fruit.

MAKES 6 SERVINGS

Preparation time: 20 minutes + 1 hour chilling

 (in mayonnaise)

¼ cup (60 mL) vegan mayonnaise such as Tofonnaise (p. 110)

2 tsp lemon juice

¼ tsp smooth Dijon mustard

1½ cups (375 mL) chopped green beans, blanched and rinsed in cold water

1 celery stalk, finely chopped

1 Gala apple, unpeeled, cored, and diced

½ cup (125 mL) toasted roughly chopped walnuts

¼ cup (60 mL) halved red grapes, seedless or seeds removed

¼ cup (60 mL) halved green grapes, seedless or seeds removed

2 tsp finely chopped capers

salt and ground black pepper, to taste

In a large bowl, combine mayonnaise, lemon juice, and mustard until mixed well.

Stir in green beans, celery, apple, walnuts, grapes, and capers. Taste and season as desired.

Chill for at least 1 hour. Bring to room temperature before serving.

Place a dollop of this salad in romaine lettuce leaves (use the tender inner leaves) or Bibb lettuce cups and serve as a summery appetizer.

Corn 'Slaw

I have Terry Hope Romero, author of Viva Vegan!, *to thank for introducing me to hominy when I was a recipe tester for that book. Now I keep trying to find new ways—like this one—to sneak it into all kinds of recipes. Be sure to let it marinate so that the hominy softens and the flavors really develop. It really is better the next day.*

MAKES 6–8 SERVINGS

Preparation time: *10 minutes + at least 2 hours chilling*

 or *(in dressing)*

1 recipe Creamy Coleslaw
   Dressing (p. 113)
1 tbsp lime juice
½ tsp ancho chili powder
   (see p. 250)
¼ tsp chili flakes
1 14-oz (398-mL) can golden or
   white hominy, drained and
   rinsed (see p. 251)
4 cups (1 L) mixed shredded
   cabbage
¾ cup (185 mL) fresh corn kernels
   (1 cob), or canned corn, rinsed,
   or thawed frozen corn
2 spring onions, finely chopped
salt and ground black pepper, to
   taste

In a large bowl, make dressing as directed. Stir in lime juice, chili powder, and chili flakes and mix to combine well. Stir in hominy. Refrigerate for at least 1 hour.

Stir in cabbage, corn kernels, and onions and mix to combine well. Chill for at least 1 more hour or overnight before serving.

Taste and season as desired.

Spicy Cumin Lime Coleslaw

Lovely when served alongside Latin-inspired dishes, this coleslaw is a little bit sweet, a little bit sour, and a little bit spicy; nicely balanced, bright, and fresh-tasting. Marinate it for as long as possible (overnight is best) to let the flavors marry and meld.

MAKES 6–8 SERVINGS

Preparation time: 20 minutes + at least 1 hour chilling

1 tsp whole cumin seeds

¼ cup (60 mL) olive oil

¼ cup (60 mL) fresh lime juice

1 tsp ground cumin

1 tbsp agave (see p. 250)

1 garlic clove, minced

½ to 1 jalapeño, minced

salt and ground black pepper, to taste

6 cups (1.5 L) shredded cabbage or coleslaw mix

½ cup (125 mL) red bell peppers, sliced into matchsticks, about ½ medium

½ cup (125 mL) thinly sliced red onions

¼ cup (60 mL) finely chopped cilantro

In a medium frying pan on medium heat, toast cumin seeds for 2 minutes, until aromatic and browned. Transfer to a large bowl.

In same large bowl, whisk in oil, lime juice, ground cumin, agave, garlic, and jalapeño until combined well. Taste and season as desired.

Add cabbage, pepper, onions, and cilantro, and toss to coat. Chill for at least 1 hour (or overnight) before serving.

Quinoa & Avocado 'Slaw

In my house, I know a dish is a success if everyone not only eats it but goes back for more. My husband is a self-proclaimed quinoa hater, but when I made this slaw along with a selection of other salads one day, it became his favorite!

MAKES 4–6 SERVINGS

Preparation time: 15 minutes, not including cooking quinoa or beans

s *(in dressing)*

n

1 recipe Creamy Coleslaw Dressing (p. 113)
½ avocado, roughly chopped
2 cups (500 mL) mixed shredded cabbage
1 cup (250 mL) cooled, cooked quinoa
½ cup (125 mL) cooked cannellini (white kidney) beans (if canned, drain and rinse)
¼ cup (60 mL) toasted pine nuts
¼ cup (60 mL) finely chopped spring onions
1 Roma tomato, seeded and diced
salt and ground black pepper, to taste

In a large bowl, make dressing as directed. Add avocado and toss to coat.

Add cabbage, quinoa, beans, nuts, onions, and tomatoes. Gently toss to coat with dressing. Chill for at least 1 hour before serving. Taste and season as desired.

Will keep, covered, for up to 2 days in refrigerator.

To yield 1 cup (250 mL) cooked quinoa, cook ⅓ cup (80 mL) quinoa in ⅔ cup (160 mL) water.

Pickle & Asparagus Potato Salad

This mayo-free potato salad bursts with flavors: sweet and sour pickles, fresh and bright asparagus, and creamy smooth potatoes. After tasting it, you may never go back to mayo-based potato salads again! (But if you do, go for the Creamy Fennel Potato Salad, p. 135.)

MAKES 4–6 SERVINGS
Preparation time: 15 minutes
Cooking time: 15 minutes + 1 hour chilling

3 cups (750 mL) cubed firm yellow potatoes, such as Yukon gold (peeling optional)

3 cups (750 mL) chopped asparagus spears, hard ends removed

3 tbsp olive oil

1 tbsp pickle juice or brining liquid

½ tsp smooth Dijon mustard

½ tsp agave (see p. 250)

¼ tsp salt

¼ tsp ground black pepper

2 tbsp finely chopped dill pickles

2 tbsp finely chopped bread-and-butter pickles

1 garlic clove, minced

1 small shallot, minced

salt and ground black pepper, to taste

In a medium saucepan fitted with a steamer basket, steam potatoes for 8–10 minutes, until fork tender. Refresh under cold running water, drain, and cool to room temperature.

In same pan, steam asparagus for 2–3 minutes, until tender. Refresh under cold running water, drain, and cool to room temperature.

In a large bowl, whisk together oil, brine, mustard, agave, salt, and pepper until well emulsified. Stir in pickles, garlic, and shallots. Add potatoes and asparagus and toss to coat. Cover and chill for at least 1 hour.

Taste and season as desired before serving.

Peanut Potato Salad

I go through spells of wanting peanut butter at every meal on everything! (Is it just me?) This recipe was created during one of these episodes. It's especially good the next day, after all the flavors have had a chance to blend and be absorbed by the potatoes.

MAKES 4–6 SERVINGS

Preparation time: 30 minutes + at least 1 hour chilling

3 medium white potatoes, cubed (peeling optional)

1 garlic clove, minced

2 tbsp smooth peanut butter

1 tsp smooth Dijon mustard

1 tbsp lemon juice

1 tsp agave (see p. 250)

¼ tsp smoked paprika

salt and ground black pepper, to taste

1 shallot, finely chopped

½ cup (125 mL) chopped red bell peppers

¼ cup (60 mL) roasted salted peanuts

1 tbsp finely chopped cilantro or spring onions, to garnish

In a medium saucepan on high heat, cover potatoes with water and bring to a boil. Reduce heat to a simmer and cook, uncovered, for 10 minutes, until fork tender.

Meanwhile, in a large bowl, whisk together garlic, peanut butter, mustard, lemon juice, 2 tbsp water, agave, and paprika. Taste and season as desired.

Drain potatoes and refresh under cold water until cool to the touch. Add potatoes, shallots, bell peppers, and peanuts to dressing and toss to coat.

Chill for at least 1 hour (best overnight) before serving. Garnish with cilantro or spring onions.

Note: The dressing may look too watery at first, but the potatoes will absorb most of the liquid.

For a spicier Peanut Potato Salad, use lime juice instead of lemon juice and add 1 finely chopped jalapeño and ½ tsp chili flakes.

Creamy Fennel Potato Salad

I put a different spin on traditional mayo-based potato salads by incorporating the anise-like flavor of fennel in this dish.

MAKES 4–6 SERVINGS
Preparation time: 5 minutes
Cooking time: 20 minutes

n *(in Chees-y Mix)*

s *(in dressing)*

3 medium Yukon gold potatoes, cubed (peeling optional)
1 tbsp grapeseed oil
2 garlic cloves, minced
1 shallot, minced
1 small fennel bulb, fronds removed, quartered, and thinly sliced
1 tbsp Dry Chees-y Mix (p. 18)
¼ cup (60 mL) Creamy Coleslaw Dressing (p. 113)
¼ cup (60 mL) finely chopped spring onions, 2 medium
¼ cup (60 mL) finely chopped fresh parsley
salt and ground black pepper, to taste

In a medium saucepan on high heat, cover potatoes with water and bring to a boil. Cook, uncovered, for 10–12 minutes, until fork tender. Drain and refresh under cold water until cool.

In same saucepan on medium-high, heat oil. Sauté garlic, shallots, and fennel for 3–4 minutes, until lightly browned. Remove from heat and cool for 5 minutes.

In a large bowl, whisk together Chees-y Mix, dressing, spring onions, parsley, and 2 tbsp water.

Add cooled potatoes and fennel and toss to combine. Taste and season as desired.

Peanut Rice Noodle Salad

This is like a cold Pad Thai; that quintessential Thai dish was the inspiration for this one. Serve with Pan Pacific Tofu (p. 161) to make a complete and completely delightful al fresco meal.

MAKES 4–6 SERVINGS

Preparation time: 20 minutes + 1 hour chilling + 20 minutes to bring to room temperature

4 oz (115 g) medium-width rice noodles, broken in half (see p. 252)

1 tbsp peanut oil

2 tbsp lime juice

1 tbsp Thai sweet chili sauce (see p. 252)

1 tbsp smooth peanut butter

2 tsp soy sauce

½–1 tsp Sriracha or other Asian hot sauce, to taste

1 garlic clove, minced

1 tsp sugar

salt and ground black pepper, to taste

1 cup (250 mL) mung bean sprouts

¼ cup (60 mL) finely chopped spring onions

¼ cup (60 mL) finely chopped red bell peppers

¼ cup (60 mL) finely chopped green bell peppers

¼ cup (60 mL) shredded carrots

¼ cup (60 mL) roasted salted peanuts

¼ cup (60 mL) roasted salted peanuts, to garnish

4–6 lime wedges

Prepare noodles according to package directions. Cool under running cold water.

In a large bowl, whisk together oil, lime juice, chili sauce, peanut butter, soy sauce, hot sauce, garlic, and sugar until combined well. Taste and season as desired. Add bean sprouts, spring onions, bell peppers, carrots, and peanuts and toss to coat. Add cooked noodles and toss to coat and combine.

Chill for at least 1 hour. Bring to room temperature before serving. Garnish with roasted peanuts and serve with lime wedges to squeeze over.

Smoky Soba Noodle Salad

This savory, smoky salad is substantial enough to serve as a meal in a bowl: grains—got it (noodles); protein—got it (tofu); vegetables—got it (bok choi); healthy fats—got it (sesame seeds and tahini). Note: Don't chill for longer than specified or noodles will clump together.

MAKES 6 SERVINGS

Preparation time: 30 minutes + 1 hour chilling

 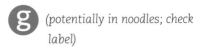

(potentially in noodles; check label)

6 oz (175 g) soba noodles, broken in half (see p. 252)

1 tbsp light miso paste (see p. 251)

1 tsp tahini (see p. 252)

¼ tsp liquid smoke

½ cup (125 mL) diced smoked tofu

2 tbsp sesame seeds

1 tbsp sesame oil

2 garlic cloves, minced

1 tbsp grated fresh ginger

2 cups (500 mL) finely chopped baby bok choi, leaves and stems separated

¼ cup (60 mL) finely chopped spring onions, about 2 medium

Prepare noodles according to package directions. Cool under running cold water.

In a large bowl, whisk together miso paste, tahini, 1 tbsp water, and liquid smoke until smooth.

In a large frying pan on medium heat, dry sauté tofu cubes for 3–4 minutes until golden, turning frequently to ensure all sides are cooked. Remove from pan and add to dressing.

In same pan, toast sesame seeds for 2 minutes, until golden. Stir into mixture in bowl.

Heat sesame oil in same frying pan. Add garlic and ginger and let sizzle. Stir in bok choi stems and sauté 2–3 minutes to soften. Remove from heat and toss bok choi leaves in pan to lightly wilt. Add to mixture in bowl along with cooked soba noodles and spring onions. Toss to coat and combine well.

Chill for 1 hour before serving.

Garlic Breadsticks (p. 185))

Smoky Soba Noodle Salad (p. 137)

Israeli Couscous Tabouleh (opposite)

Israeli Couscous Tabouleh

What on earth can you do when your garden is producing copious amounts of parsley? Make this refreshing version of the quintessential Middle Eastern salad! I use oversized Israeli couscous instead of bulgur wheat, which gives it a slightly different mouth feel than more traditional tabouleh.

MAKES 4 SERVINGS
Preparation time: 20 minutes
Cooking time: 25 minutes + 1 hour chilling

2 tbsp olive oil

2 garlic cloves, minced

2 shallots, finely chopped

½ cup (125 mL) finely chopped fresh parsley stalks

1 tsp ground cumin

½ tsp dried oregano

¼ tsp dried marjoram

1 cup (250 mL) uncooked Israeli couscous

1¼ cups (310 mL) vegetable stock

2 tbsp lemon juice

1 cup (250 mL) loosely packed, finely chopped fresh flat (Italian) parsley leaves

1 cup (250 mL) loosely packed, finely chopped fresh curly (plain) parsley leaves

⅓ cup (80 mL) firmly packed, finely chopped fresh mint leaves

½ cup (125 mL) finely diced, seeded tomato

½ cup (125 mL) finely diced, seeded cucumber (peeling optional)

salt and ground black pepper, to taste

In a large frying pan on medium, heat oil. Sauté garlic, shallots, and parsley stalks for 5 minutes, until stalks softened. Add cumin, oregano, and marjoram and sauté 1 minute more. Add couscous and toast for 2 minutes, until aromatic.

Add stock, stir, cover, and cook for 10 minutes, until liquid is absorbed. Remove from heat, stir in lemon juice, cover, and let sit for 5 minutes.

Stir in parsley, mint, tomatoes, and cucumbers. Taste and season as desired.

Transfer to a serving bowl and chill for at least 1 hour before serving.

Creamy Macaroni Salad

This is my version of the traditional macaroni salad, found at every barbecue, picnic, and potluck. Of course, I like my version best (it's the artichoke hearts!) and I hope you enjoy it too.

MAKES 4–6 SERVINGS

Preparation time: *10 minutes, not including cooking macaroni + 1 hour chilling*

g *(in pasta only)*

s or **n** *(in mayonnaise)*

½ cup (125 mL) vegan mayonnaise such as Tofonnaise (p. 110)

2 canned artichoke hearts, drained and rinsed, roughly chopped

1 garlic clove, minced

½ tsp garlic powder

½ tsp onion powder

½ tsp salt

¼ tsp white pepper

1 tsp agave (see p. 250)

1 tsp white balsamic vinegar (see p. 252)

1 celery stalk, finely chopped

¼ cup (60 mL) finely chopped green bell peppers

¼ cup (60 mL) finely chopped red or orange bell peppers

2 tbsp finely chopped bread-and-butter pickles

4 cups (1 L) cold, cooked macaroni (gluten-free if desired)

salt and ground black pepper, to taste

In a food processor or blender, pulse together mayonnaise, artichokes, garlic, garlic powder, onion powder, salt, white pepper, agave, and vinegar until smooth and creamy. Stop to scrape sides of bowl as required.

Transfer to a large bowl and stir in celery, bell peppers, pickles, and macaroni. Taste and season as desired.

Chill for 1 hour before serving.

Variations on the theme:

• Add 1½ cups (375 mL) or 1 14-oz (398-mL) can cooked chickpeas.

• Substitute ripe and creamy avocado for mayonnaise.

• Add a minced jalapeño if you like it spicy!

Millet & Broccoli Salad

In this mellow, mustard-y salad, the broccoli is enhanced by the vibrancy of the dressing, and the millet is a neutral backdrop allowing all the flavors to shine. Even those members of my family who aren't really millet fans (you know who you are) love this salad. Note: You can substitute other grains, such as quinoa or brown rice, for the millet.

MAKES 4–6 SERVINGS

Preparation time: 10 minutes, not including cooking times for millet or broccoli + 1 hour chilling

n *(in Chees-y Mix)*

1 tbsp tahini (see p. 252)
1 tbsp prepared yellow mustard
2 tbsp lemon juice
1½ tbsp Dry Chees-y Mix (p. 18)
1 cup (250 mL) cooked cannellini (white kidney) beans (if canned, drained and rinsed)
2 cups (500 mL) cooked, cooled broccoli florets
1½ cups (375 mL) cooked, cooled millet
2 spring onions, finely chopped
salt and ground black pepper, to taste

In a large bowl, whisk together the tahini, mustard, lemon juice, and Chees-y Mix. Add beans, broccoli, millet, and spring onions. Toss to coat. Taste and season as desired.

Chill for at least 1 hour before serving.

To yield 1½ cups cooked millet, cook ½ cup (125 mL) millet in 1¼ cups (310 mL) water or stock.

Fennel & Wild Rice Salad

The fennel in this salad is caramelized and sweet—it's difficult not to stand in the kitchen and eat it straight from the pan when it comes out of the oven!

MAKES 4 SERVINGS

Preparation time: 45 minutes, *including roasting time*

2 medium fennel bulbs, halved and trimmed

1 tbsp olive oil (for fennel)

1 tsp balsamic vinegar (for fennel)

salt and ground black pepper, to taste

1 tbsp olive oil (for dressing)

1 tsp balsamic vinegar (for dressing)

½ tsp smooth Dijon mustard

1 garlic clove, minced

1 cup (250 mL) cooked, cooled wild rice

¼ cup (60 mL) finely chopped spring onions, about 2 medium

¼ cup (60 mL) shredded fresh basil

Preheat oven or barbecue to 425°F (220°C).

Slice fennel into ¼-in (6-mm) wide strips. In a large bowl, toss fennel with oil and vinegar.

Spread in a single layer on a large roasting pan or piece of foil if grilling on barbecue and sprinkle with a little salt and pepper. Roast for 25–30 minutes, until golden and lightly caramelized. Cool to room temperature.

While fennel roasts, in same bowl, whisk together oil, vinegar, mustard, garlic, and a little salt and pepper. Add cooked rice, spring onions, and basil and toss to coat.

Chill for 30 minutes until fennel has roasted and cooled. Toss fennel with dressed rice.

Southwestern Spelt Salad

In this salad, the spelt berries (whole unrefined grains) are chewy and a little sweet, the beans are soft and creamy, the vegetables crisp and crunchy, and the dressing a little tart—a very tempting combination.

MAKES 6–8 SERVINGS

Preparation time: 10 minutes, not including time for cooking spelt and beans + 1 hour chilling

2½ tbsp fresh lime juice

2 tsp agave (see p. 250)

1 tsp soy sauce

½ tsp liquid smoke

¼ tsp garlic powder

¼ tsp salt

dash hot sauce, to taste

2¼ (560 mL) cups cooked spelt berries, room temperature

¾ cup (185 mL) corn kernels (1 cob) (if canned, drain and rinse)

½ cup (125 mL) cooked black beans (if canned, drain and rinse)

½ cup (125 mL) finely chopped red onions

½ cup (125 mL) finely chopped red bell peppers

⅓ cup (80 mL) finely chopped cilantro

salt and ground black pepper, to taste

In a large bowl, whisk together lime juice, agave, soy sauce, liquid smoke, garlic powder, salt, and hot sauce. Taste and season as desired.

Stir in spelt, corn, beans, onions, bell peppers, and cilantro and toss to coat.

Chill for at least 1 hour. Taste and adjust seasoning if necessary before serving.

To yield 2¼ cups (560 mL) cooked spelt berries, cook 1 cup (250 mL) uncooked spelt berries in 2½ cups (625 mL) water. You can use wheat berries instead.

Roasted Beet & Quinoa Salad

Beets, especially if they are roasted to bring out their natural sweetness, always add an earthy touch to a dish. In this salad, they are paired with nutty quinoa and lifted by the slight bitterness of the greens. If you can't find beets with greens attached, use another slightly bitter green such as arugula.

MAKES 6 SERVINGS

Preparation time: 60 minutes, including roasting time

3 medium beets, any color, with greens attached

2 tbsp olive oil

1 tbsp white balsamic vinegar (see p. 252)

salt and ground black pepper, to taste

¼ cup (60 mL) white wine or vegetable stock

1 tbsp olive oil

1 tsp smooth Dijon mustard

½ tsp garlic powder

½ tsp onion powder

½ cup (125 mL) finely chopped red bell peppers

¼ cup (60 mL) finely chopped red onions

1 cup (250 mL) cooked and cooled white or red quinoa

Preheat oven to 425°F (220°C).

Remove greens from beets and set aside in refrigerator. Peel and cube beets.

On a roasting pan, toss beets with 2 tbsp olive oil, vinegar, and a little salt and pepper. Roast beets for 40–45 minutes, until tender and slightly caramelized. Set aside beets in a large bowl, then deglaze pan with white wine. Add liquid, after deglazing, to bowl. Cool to room temperature.

In a large bowl, whisk in 1 tbsp oil, mustard, garlic powder, and onion powder. Add bell peppers, onions, quinoa, and beets and toss to combine. Shred beet greens and lightly toss to combine.

Serve at room temperature.

Hearty Three-Grain Salad

If you've got leftover spelt berries from the Southwestern Spelt Salad recipe (p. 143), leftover brown rice from last night's dinner, and some barley in the cupboard, here's a hearty salad to the rescue! Chewy grains, crunchy vegetables, and a hint of raspberries, this is a perfect picnic salad on a hot summer's day.

MAKES 6 SERVINGS

Preparation time: 15 minutes, not including time to cook grains + 1 hour chilling

½ cup (125 mL) fresh raspberries

1 garlic clove, minced

1 tsp grated fresh ginger

2 tbsp grapeseed oil

1 tbsp lemon juice

salt and ground black pepper, to taste

1 celery stalk, finely chopped

½ medium carrot, finely chopped

¼ cup (60 mL) finely chopped red onions

3 tbsp dried cranberries

1 cup (250 mL) cooked, cooled long-grain brown rice

1 cup (250 mL) cooked, cooled barley, rinsed well

1 cup (250 mL) cooked, cooled spelt or wheat berries

Over a large bowl, press raspberries through a sieve. Reserve liquid and discard seeds.

Stir in garlic, ginger, oil, and lemon juice and whisk to combine. Taste and season as desired.

Stir in celery, carrots, onions, and cranberries and toss to coat. Stir in cooked grains and combine well.

Chill for at least 1 hour before serving.

Fresh Fruit Salad Q & A

Fruit salads are best made not more than 1–2 hours before serving, so the flavors have time enough to meld, but the fruit doesn't have a chance to get mushy. Transport to your picnic in a large bowl with a resealable lid (that won't leak on the way) and refrigerate until it's time to pack the cooler, to reduce oxidation and spoilage. Return to room temperature before serving.

Q: What can I serve with fruit salad?
A: It's always good on its own, but if you need something, I recommend Vanilla Ice Cream (p. 206)—unless you're at a picnic away from home, as ice cream doesn't travel well.

Q: What should I do with any leftovers?
A: Add a banana and some juice or soy milk and blend until smooth for an instant fruit smoothie. If you like, freeze the smoothie in ice-pop molds for a frozen fruity treat.

Q: What kinds of fruit should I use?
A: Good fruits include:

- stone fruit: peaches, nectarines, apricots
- melons: cantaloupe, honeydew, watermelon
- grapes: red, green (seedless varieties are best)
- berries: raspberries, strawberries, blueberries, blackberries
- tropical fruit: pineapple, mango, kiwifruit, papaya
- citrus fruit: oranges, grapefruits, clementines/mandarin oranges
- fresh figs

Remove pits, cut to roughly uniform pieces, and remove flawed or bruised parts. Peeling is optional. You can also add canned fruit.

Q: What kinds of fruit should I avoid?
A: Bananas don't last well in fruit salads, especially in hot summer conditions—not only do they go brown, but they tend to become mushy. If you do use sliced bananas, sprinkle with a little lime or lemon juice and add at the last minute. Apples and pears also need a lemon or lime juice drizzle to prevent discoloration. Add these at the last minute too.

Q: What kinds of fruits go together well?
A: I like to create a fruit family theme, such as a melon salad with a variety of melons and a touch of fresh mint leaves. Mixed berry salad with shredded basil and a touch of white balsamic vinegar is also good.

Q: Can I add other things to fruit salad?
A: Add small amounts of just 1 of the following ingredients:

- shredded fresh mint leaves
- shredded fresh basil leaves
- crushed lemongrass stalks (remove before serving)
- lime or lemon zest
- small dried fruits such as cranberries, blueberries, or raisins
- cinnamon, either as a stick or ground and sprinkled on top
- dried coconut flakes (unsweetened)

Q: How can I adjust the sweetness or tartness of the fruit salad?
A: If the fruit isn't as sweet as you'd hoped, add a little agave and stir through. If it is too sweet, add a little lemon or lime juice or white balsamic vinegar. A pinch of salt sprinkled over the fruit will lift all the flavors.

THE RECIPES THAT FOLLOW ARE *mainly (though by no means all) entrées, the protein heart of a meal. I have used a variety of vegan protein sources, from tofu, tempeh, and seitan to nuts, seeds, and beans, to suit a variety of tastes and tolerances. The flavorings are numerous and varied, from smoky traditional barbecue to Asian-inspired, Mexican-inspired, and downright fusion! In this chapter you'll also find some delectable vegetable recipes which, while perfect as stand-alone dishes, are equally at home as sides. Most of these recipes are meant to be cooked al fresco on a barbecue, but you may use a frying pan on the stovetop or a broiler or bake them in a hot oven without oil, but cooking times and end results may vary from those given here.*

on the grill

Chipotle & Cilantro Lentil Burgers

This recipe makes a large amount, so if you're not feeding a crowd at your cookout, know that these burgers freeze well. I use Puy (French green) lentils as they hold their shape without becoming too soggy. Serve these on buns with lettuce, tomato slices, and a sprinkle of Massaged Red Onions & Cumin (p. 84) for a taste sensation.

MAKES 9 SERVINGS
Preparation time: *20 minutes, + 1 hour chilling*
Cooking time: *10 minutes*

1½ tsp whole cumin seeds
1½ tsp coriander seeds, partially crushed
1 tbsp olive oil
1 medium onion, finely chopped
2 garlic cloves, minced
2 celery stalks, finely chopped
¼ cup (60 mL) finely chopped cilantro stalks
4 cups (1 L) cooked Puy or beluga lentils
½ cup (125 mL) chopped cilantro leaves
1 chipotle in adobo sauce, seeded (see p. 250)
1 tbsp tomato paste
1 tsp liquid smoke
1 tsp ground cumin
½ tsp salt
½ tsp dried basil
½ tsp dried oregano
1 cup (250 mL) cooked Puy or beluga lentils
⅔ cup (160 mL) quinoa or millet flour (see p. 251)

In a large non-stick frying pan on medium heat, toast seeds for 2–3 minutes, stirring frequently, until aromatic. Remove from heat and place in a large mixing bowl.

In same pan, heat oil. Sauté onions, garlic, celery, and cilantro stalks for 10 minutes, until very soft and lightly browned. Remove from heat and add to toasted seeds.

In a food processor, blend cooked lentils, cilantro leaves, chipotle, tomato paste, liquid smoke, cumin, salt, basil, and oregano until completely smooth. Stop to scrape sides of bowl as required. Stir into vegetable and seed mixture.

Stir in 1 cup (250 mL) unblended lentils and flour and mix to combine well.

Using a ⅓ cup (80 mL) scoop, portion mixture into 9 burger patties about 3-in (8-cm) in diameter. Chill for at least 1 hour before cooking.

Preheat lightly oiled barbecue to medium heat. For a clean grill, lay down a sheet of aluminum foil lightly brushed with oil.

Grill on medium heat for 5 minutes per side until browned. Turn only once for best results.

To yield 5 cups (1.25 L) cooked lentils, cook 2 cups (500 mL) dry lentils in enough water to cover.

Beet & Bean Burgers

These burgers have such a vibrant color and dense hearty texture that they really hit the spot when you're hungering for something "meaty." They're great on a bun topped with a light, refreshing dressing, such as the Tangy Lemon Sour Cream Dressing (p. 117), and fresh lettuce leaves.

MAKES 8 SERVINGS

Preparation time: 25 minutes + 1 hour chilling
Cooking time: 10 minutes

3 cups (750 mL) peeled and grated beets

1 cup (250 mL) cooked adzuki or black beans (if canned, drain and rinse)

½ onion, grated

2 garlic cloves, grated

1 tbsp tomato paste

1 tsp Marmite or liquid smoke (see p. 251)

½ tsp ground fennel seeds

½ tsp ground caraway seeds

½ tsp salt

¼ tsp ground black pepper

¾ cup (185 mL) quick-cooking rolled oats

¾ cup (185 mL) breadcrumbs (gluten-free if desired)

salt and ground black pepper, to taste

In a medium saucepan on medium heat, cook grated beets in enough water to cover, uncovered, for 12 minutes, until tender. Drain and squeeze all liquid out of beets through a strainer with the back of a wooden spoon. Return beets to saucepan and let sit for 10 minutes to cool.

Stir in beans, onions, garlic, tomato paste, Marmite, fennel seeds, caraway seeds, salt, and pepper. Mash ingredients thoroughly with a potato masher. Add oats and breadcrumbs and mix well with a wooden spoon. Taste and season as desired.

Using a ⅓ cup (80 mL) scoop, portion mixture into 8 3-in (8-cm) burger patties. Chill for at least 1 hour before cooking.

Preheat barbecue to medium–medium-high heat. Lay down a sheet of aluminum foil lightly brushed with oil.

Grill burgers 5 minutes on each side, until lightly browned.

Groovy Multi-Grain Burgers

Substantial and filling, these burgers are filled with a multitude of grains in a variety of forms. The textures and flavors of each are complementary, and you'll find they mesh together perfectly. Serve them with the Spicy Cumin Lime Coleslaw (p. 130).

MAKES 6 SERVINGS

Preparation time: 45 minutes + 1 hour chilling

Cooking time: 10 minutes

1 tbsp olive oil

½ medium onion, finely chopped

2 garlic cloves, minced

1 small celery stalk, finely chopped

1 tsp Faux Poultry Seasoning Mix (p. 19)

½ tsp salt

¼ tsp chili flakes

¼ cup (60 mL) finely chopped carrots

¼ cup (60 mL) finely chopped broccoli stalks

½ cup (125 mL) vegetable stock

1 bay leaf

¼ cup (60 mL) whole amaranth (see p. 250)

¾ cup (185 mL) cooked long-grain brown rice, room temperature

½ cup (125 mL) quick-cooking rolled oats

¼ cup (60 mL) white rice flour (see p. 251)

¼ cup (60 mL) millet flour (see p. 251)

1 tbsp cornstarch

3–6 tbsp vegetable stock

salt and ground black pepper, to taste

In a medium frying pan on medium, heat oil. Sauté onions, garlic, and celery for 5 minutes, until soft and translucent. Add seasoning mix, salt, and chili flakes and sauté 1 more minute.

Stir in carrots and broccoli and sauté for 3–4 minutes, until a little softened. Stir in ½ cup (125 mL) stock and bay leaf and bring to a boil. Stir in amaranth and reduce heat to medium-low. Cover pan and simmer for 25 minutes, until liquid is mostly absorbed and grains are tender and thick. Remove from heat, uncover, and stir. Refrigerate for 10 minutes or cool on countertop for 30 minutes, until room temperature.

Line a large plate with parchment or cling film.

Remove amaranth mixture from refrigerator. Remove bay leaf and stir in brown rice and rolled oats.

Stir in flours and cornstarch. Add 3–6 tbsp stock 1 tbsp at a time until mixture is sticky, damp but not overly wet, and holds together when pressed. Taste and season as desired.

With dampened hands, divide mixture into 6 equal portions and form into burger patties. Place on prepared plate, cover, and chill for at least 1 hour.

Preheat barbecue to medium heat. Lay down a sheet of aluminum foil lightly brushed with oil.

Cook burgers for 4–5 minutes per side until both sides are golden brown, turning once.

Seitan Burgers (opposite)

Chili & Tomato Jam (p. 81)

Corn & Olive Foccacia (p. 187)

Seitan Burgers

These thick, chewy burgers maintain their moistness after grilling and are great in a bun topped with lettuce, tomatoes, and pickles. Serve with mounds of Pickle & Asparagus Potato Salad (p. 132) and/or Spicy Cumin Lime Coleslaw (p. 130) on the side. Best when prepared a day in advance of grilling.

MAKES 8–10 SERVINGS

Preparation time: 20 minutes
Cooking time: 90 minutes + grilling

¼ cup (60 mL) tomato paste

1 tbsp liquid smoke

1 tbsp maple syrup

2 tbsp soy sauce

2 garlic cloves, minced

½ cup (125 mL) TVP granules (see p. 252)

¼ cup (60 mL) + 1 tbsp vegetable stock

½ cup (125 mL) nutritional yeast (see p. 251)

2 tsp onion powder

2 tsp garlic powder

1 tsp smoked paprika

½ tsp white pepper

½ tsp ground sage

½ tsp dried thyme

¼ tsp salt

1½ cups (375 mL) vital wheat gluten powder (see p. 252)

....

Preheat oven or barbecue to 325°F (160°C). Ready a large baking sheet and a large (about 14-in or 35-cm long) sheet of aluminum foil.

In a large bowl, whisk to combine ¾ cup (185 mL) boiling water, tomato paste, liquid smoke, maple syrup, soy sauce, and garlic. Stir in TVP granules, cover, and let sit for 15 minutes.

Stir in vegetable stock, nutritional yeast, onion powder, garlic powder, paprika, white pepper, sage, thyme, salt, and reconstituted vital wheat gluten.

Knead in bowl for 1 minute to work in gluten. Turn onto a clean board and knead for 2–3 minutes to further activate gluten.

Shape into a log about 5 in (12 cm) long and 4 in (10 cm) in diameter. Wrap in aluminum foil, tucking in ends. Place on baking sheet. Bake for 85–90 minutes, turning after 45 minutes to help maintain round shape, until firm to the touch and very aromatic.

Cool for 15–20 minutes, then unwrap. Cool completely.

At this stage, log can be refrigerated in 1 piece for up to 3 days. Sliced burgers can be individually wrapped in cling film and frozen for up to 1 month. Thaw completely before cooking.

When ready to grill, slice into ½–¾-in (1–2-cm) thick slices.

Preheat a lightly oiled barbecue to medium-high heat. For a clean grill, lay down a sheet of aluminum foil lightly brushed with oil.

Cook burgers 3–5 minutes on each side, until browned.

For more information on seitan, see p. 252.

Super Seed Burgers

These are firm-textured burgers that hold together well for grilling, broiling, baking, pan frying— however you want to cook them. I adore these topped with Fresh Tomato & Pepper Salsa (p. 76), or Chili & Tomato Jam (p. 81).

MAKES 8 SERVINGS

*Preparation time: 30 minutes +
1 hour chilling*
Cooking time: 10 minutes

1 tbsp ground chia seeds
(see p. 250)

1 tbsp olive oil

½ onion, finely chopped

2 garlic cloves, minced

1 shallot, finely chopped

1 celery stalk, finely chopped

½ cup (125 mL) raw pine nuts

½ cup (125 mL) raw sunflower
seeds

½ cup (125 mL) raw pumpkin
seeds

¼ cup (60 mL) hemp seeds
(see p. 251)

½ cup (125 mL) chickpea flour,
sifted if lumpy (see p. 251)

3 tbsp ground flaxseeds

2 tbsp sesame seeds

1 tbsp poppy seeds

1 tsp salt

1 tsp dried oregano

½ tsp ground fennel seeds

½ tsp ground caraway seeds

½ tsp ground star anise seeds

½ tsp dried thyme

½ tsp ground white pepper

¼ cup (60 mL) tahini (see p. 252)

2 tbsp olive oil

¼ cup (60 mL) vegetable stock

In a medium bowl, stir chia seeds into ¼ cup (60 mL) + 2 tbsp water with a fork. Let sit for 15 minutes.

In a large frying pan on medium, heat oil. Sauté onions, garlic, shallots, and celery for 10 minutes, until soft but not browned. Remove from heat and set aside.

In a food processor, pulse to combine pine nuts and sunflower, pumpkin, and hemp seeds, until mix resembles a coarse meal. Stir into vegetable mixture.

Stir in chickpea flour, flaxseeds, sesame seeds, poppy seeds, salt, oregano, fennel seeds, caraway seeds, star anise seeds, thyme, and pepper.

Add tahini, oil, and stock to reconstituted chia seeds and whisk with a fork to combine. Stir into seed and vegetable mixture to combine well.

With dampened hands, shape mixture into 8 burger patties. Chill for at least 1 hour.

Preheat barbecue to medium heat. Lay down a sheet of aluminum foil lightly brushed with oil.

Grill patties for 3–5 minutes each side on foil until golden with a crisp crust. Be careful when flipping burgers, as they may stick.

The burger patties may look a little too wet before chilling, but will firm up and absorb the extra moisture in the refrigerator. No need to add extra flour!

Gluten-free Chickpea Sausages

Now all your gluten-free friends can enjoy grilled sausages too! These are not as firm or sturdy as those containing vital wheat gluten, but they do hold together and crisp up nicely. Great for the grill or pan-frying.

MAKES 4 SERVINGS

Preparation time: 45 minutes +
1 hour chilling
Cooking time: 60 minutes +
10 minutes grilling

½ cup (125 mL) vegetable stock

2 tbsp ground flaxseeds

2 tbsp ground chia seeds
(see p. 250)

1¼ cup (310 mL) cooked chickpeas
(if canned, drain and rinse)

3 tbsp olive oil

¼ tsp salt

½ tsp garlic powder

½ tsp onion powder

½ tsp dried thyme

¼ tsp ground black pepper

⅛ tsp ground fennel seeds

⅛ tsp paprika

¼ cup (60 mL) nutritional yeast
(see p. 251)

½ cup (125 mL) chickpea flour,
sifted if lumpy (see p. 251)

In a medium bowl, combine stock, flaxseeds, and chia seeds. Let sit for 10 minutes to thicken.

In a food processor, blend chickpeas, oil, salt, garlic powder, onion powder, thyme, pepper, fennel seeds, and paprika until smooth. Add nutritional yeast, chickpea flour, and flaxseed mixture and pulse to combine well. Place food processor bowl in refrigerator to chill for 30 minutes.

Place a collapsible steam basket in a large saucepan. Add water to reach bottom of basket. Prepare 4 8-in (20-cm) lengths of aluminum foil. With dampened hands, divide mixture into 4 equal pieces and shape into logs about 5 in (12 cm) long and about 1 in (2.5 cm) in diameter. (The mixture is very soft.)

Wrap each log firmly in aluminum foil. Twist ends to seal. Place wrapped logs in steamer basket.

Cover saucepan and on high heat, bring water to a boil. Reduce heat to medium-low. Cook for 60 minutes until sausages are firm to the touch. Check water level periodically and top up as needed.

Remove from heat. Cool sausages to room temperature.

Chill for at least 1 hour to continue firming.

Preheat a lightly oiled barbecue to medium–medium-high heat. (For a clean grill, lay down a sheet of aluminum foil lightly brushed with oil.)

Grill sausages for 10 minutes in total, until golden on all sides.

Shape mixture into burger patties for Gluten-free Chickpea Burgers.

Garlic & Sage Sausages

Be warned: these sausages are pretty garlicky! They do mellow after cooking, and the enough-to-frighten-a-vampire amount of garlic will sweetly sing in combination with the sage and other spices.

MAKES 4 SERVINGS
Preparation time: 20 minutes
Cooking time: 60 minutes + 10 minutes grilling

1 cup (250 mL) cooked cannellini (white kidney) beans

1 garlic clove, finely chopped

½ celery stalk, finely chopped

4 cloves Stovetop Poached Garlic (p. 21)

2½ tbsp Garlic-Infused Oil (p. 21), or olive oil

1 tsp garlic powder

1 tsp ground sage

½ tsp onion powder

½ tsp dried thyme

½ tsp salt

¼ tsp ground black pepper

2 tbsp dry breadcrumbs

½ cup (125 mL) + 2 tbsp vegetable stock

¼ cup (60 mL) nutritional yeast (see p. 251)

1 cup (250 mL) vital wheat gluten powder (see p. 252)

....

Place a collapsible steam basket in a large saucepan. Add water to reach bottom of basket. Prepare 4 8-in (20-cm) lengths of aluminum foil.

In a food processor, pulse to combine beans, garlic, celery, and poached garlic. Add oil, garlic powder, sage, onion powder, thyme, salt, and pepper and blend until smooth with no lumps. Stop to scrape down sides of bowl as required.

Add breadcrumbs and pulse to combine well. Texture should be thick and smooth, yet moist to the touch.

Transfer to a large bowl and stir in stock. Stir in nutritional yeast and mix to combine well. Stir in gluten and mix well with fork. Knead in bowl for 3–4 minutes to activate gluten.

Divide into 4 equal pieces and shape into logs about 5 in (12 cm) long and about 1 in (2.5 cm) in diameter. Wrap each log firmly in aluminum foil. Twist ends to seal.

Place wrapped logs in steamer basket. Cover saucepan and on high heat, bring water to a boil. Reduce heat to medium-low. Cook for 60 minutes, until sausages are firm to the touch. Check water level periodically and top up as needed.

Remove from heat. Let cool, then unwrap. If not using immediately, cool to room temperature before storing in refrigerator for up to 1 week.

Preheat a barbecue to medium–medium-high heat. Lay down a sheet of aluminum foil lightly brushed with oil.

Grill sausages for 10 minutes in total, turning frequently until golden and slightly crispy.

Pan Pacific Tofu

In this summer-ific recipe, tofu is coated in a sweet and spicy marinade that infuses it with flavors from Southeast Asia. You can travel without leaving home!

MAKES 4 SERVINGS
Preparation time: 5 minutes + 1 hour marinating
Cooking time: 15 minutes

3 tbsp soy sauce

2 tbsp lime juice

2 tbsp canola oil

2 tbsp agave (see p. 250)

1 garlic clove, minced

1 tbsp rice wine vinegar

1 tbsp Thai sweet chili sauce (see p. 252)

1 tsp Sriracha or other Asian hot sauce, or to taste

1 tbsp finely chopped cilantro

1 tsp lime zest

½ tsp ground cumin

salt and ground black pepper, to taste

1 lb (500 g) extra-firm regular tofu (water-packed), sliced widthwise into 12 equal slices

In a large flat container with resealable lid or in a ziplock bag, combine soy sauce, lime juice, oil, agave, garlic, vinegar, chili sauce, hot sauce, cilantro, lime zest, and cumin. Taste marinade and season as desired.

Add tofu slices and marinate for at least 1 hour, turning after 30 minutes.

Preheat barbecue to medium heat. Lay down a sheet of aluminum foil lightly brushed with oil. Grill tofu for 5 minutes per side, basting frequently with leftover marinade.

Mojito-Inspired Tofu

My husband is a restaurant manager, and one day he had to spend eight hours making mojitos at a charity golf tournament his restaurant sponsored. His unfortunate experience inspired me to use the refreshing Latino flavors of the mojito as a delectable marinade and basting sauce for barbecued tofu. Bad for him, good for the rest of us!

MAKES 4 SERVINGS

Preparation time: 5 minutes + 1 hour marinating

Cooking time: 10 minutes

¼ cup (60 mL) + 2 tbsp fresh lime juice

¼ cup (60 mL) light rum

¼ cup (60 mL) finely chopped fresh mint

1½ tbsp agave (see p. 250)

1 tbsp canola oil

2 garlic cloves, minced

2 tsp lime zest

½ tsp salt

1 lb (500 g) extra-firm regular tofu (water-packed), drained and pressed, sliced widthwise into 12 rectangles

In a large flat container with a resealable lid or in a large ziplock bag, combine juice, rum, mint, agave, oil, garlic, lime zest, and salt. Add tofu and marinate in refrigerator for at least 1 hour, turning after 30 minutes.

Preheat barbecue to medium heat. Lay down a sheet of aluminum foil lightly brushed with oil. Grill for 3–4 minutes each side until golden, basting frequently with leftover marinade.

Cedar-Planked Rosemary & Lemon Tofu

Very Pacific Northwest-inspired, this smoky barbecued tofu can be yours with the use of food-grade cedar planks. It may sound tricky, but it really isn't, and has the added bonus of keeping your grill clean!

MAKES 4 SERVINGS

Preparation time: 15 minutes + 8 hours to soak plank

Cooking time: 20 minutes

4 sprigs fresh rosemary

¼ cup (60 mL) lemon juice

2 tbsp olive oil (for marinade)

1 tsp lemon pepper

1 tbsp lemon zest

1 tbsp finely chopped fresh or
    1 tsp crushed dried rosemary

½ tsp salt

2 tbsp olive oil (for coating plank)

1 lemon, sliced

1 lb (500 g) extra-firm regular tofu
    (water-packed), sliced widthwise
    into 12 slices

salt and ground black pepper, to
    taste

....

In a large container, submerge plank in enough warm water to cover when pressed down. Add rosemary sprigs and lemon juice. Place a heavy item, such as a can of beans, on top of plank to completely submerge it. Let sit for at least 8 hours (preferably overnight) to completely soak through. Do not discard rosemary sprigs.

When ready to barbecue, in a small bowl, combine oil, lemon pepper, lemon zest, fresh or dried rosemary and salt.

Dry plank and lightly coat top surface with oil. Rub plank with rosemary sprigs.

Preheat barbecue to 350°F (180°C). Place plank on grill for 5 minutes to preheat.

Lay lemon slices on plank to create a bed for tofu. Rub tofu slices with seasoned olive oil mixture. Arrange tofu on lemon slices and season with a little salt and pepper. Reduce heat to lowest temperature so plank smolders but does not catch fire.

Close lid and cook for 30 minutes. Do not turn tofu, but check briefly every 7–10 minutes for flare-ups. Smoldering is fine, but flames are not. If plank catches fire, reduce heat further (if possible) and extinguish flames with water.

Using cedar planks

- Buy food-grade cedar planks where barbecue supplies are sold.
- Keep barbecue lid closed while cooking to capture smoke and retain heat.
- Keep a spray bottle of water on hand to extinguish flames.
- Rinse, dry, and re-use planks if not too burnt.

Lime & Ginger Tahini Tofu Skewers

One day I was craving peanut sauce, but had no peanut butter in the house. With a little imagination and some adjustments, I satisfied my peanut cravings with this creation, which is great for patio parties. The sauce is also tasty served over green vegetables.

MAKES 6 SERVINGS

Preparation time: 5 minutes + 1 hour marinating

Cooking time: 15 minutes

½ cup (125 mL) ginger ale or ginger beer

¼ cup (60 mL) lime juice

2 tbsp soy sauce

2 tbsp tahini (see p. 252)

2 tbsp agave (see p. 250)

1 tbsp grated fresh ginger

2 garlic cloves, grated or finely minced

1 lb (500 g) extra-firm regular tofu (water-packed), drained and pressed, cubed

1½ tbsp arrowroot powder (see p. 250)

In a medium saucepan, whisk to combine ginger ale, lime juice, soy sauce, tahini, agave, ginger, and garlic. Add tofu, submerge in marinade, and cover pan. Place pan in refrigerator and marinate tofu for at least 1 hour. Stir to coat well after 30 minutes.

Meanwhile, soak wooden skewers in water for 1 hour. Remove tofu from marinade and thread 6 cubes onto each skewer. Reserve marinade.

Preheat barbecue to medium heat. Lay down a sheet of aluminum foil lightly brushed with oil. Grill for 10 minutes in total, turning as required, until golden on each side.

Meanwhile, add arrowroot powder to marinade and whisk to combine. On medium heat (directly on barbecue if pan is safe for use on grill), cook marinade, whisking frequently, for 5 minutes, until thickened. Pour sauce over tofu, or serve on the side as desired.

You will need: 6 6-in (15-cm) wooden skewers for this recipe.

Maple Tofu Barbecue Skewers

I first made these for Canada Day a few years ago and I've done so every year since, even when the weather means we have to cook indoors. Seriously, what is more quintessentially Canadian than maple syrup? These are a little sweet, smoky—and really good. (For more Canada or Independence Day menu suggestions, see p. 254.)

MAKES 4 SERVINGS
Preparation time: 10 minutes + 1 hour marinating
Cooking time: 15 minutes

S

¼ cup (60 mL) maple syrup
3 tbsp soy sauce
2 tbsp canola oil
1½ tsp liquid smoke
1 garlic clove, minced
1 tsp maple extract
1 tsp garlic powder
1 tsp onion powder
¼ tsp smoked paprika
¼ tsp dried thyme
salt and ground black pepper, to taste (optional)
1 lb (500 g) extra-firm regular tofu (water-packed), drained and pressed, cubed

In a large flat container with a resealable lid or in a large ziplock bag, combine syrup, soy sauce, oil, liquid smoke, garlic, maple extract, garlic powder, onion powder, paprika, and thyme. Taste and season as desired.

Add tofu and marinate in refrigerator for at least 1 hour, turning after 30 minutes.

Meanwhile, soak skewers in water for 1 hour. Remove tofu from marinade and thread an equal number of cubes onto each skewer. Reserve marinade.

Preheat barbecue to medium heat. Lay down a sheet of aluminum foil lightly brushed with oil. Grill for 3–4 minutes on each side until golden, basting with leftover marinade when skewers are turned.

Use leftover marinade as a salad dressing by mixing with ¼ cup (125 mL) vegan mayonnaise, as a stir-fry sauce for vegetables, or as a dipping sauce.

You will need 4 12-in (25-cm) wooden skewers for this recipe.

Mango & Orange Tempeh with Ginger

Another wonderful idea for tempeh on the barbecue using mango chutney, an ingredient more often associated with Indian cuisine. Here, the flavors are all at once sweet and tart, and the tempeh is both sticky and tender.

MAKES 4 SERVINGS

Preparation time: 20 minutes + 1 hour marinating

Cooking time: 15 minutes

2 tsp apple cider vinegar

8 oz (230 g) tempeh, whole piece (see p. 252)

MARINADE

¼ cup (60 mL) fresh orange juice

3 tbsp prepared mango chutney (see p. 251)

2 garlic cloves, minced

1 tbsp lemon juice

1 tbsp grated fresh ginger

1 tbsp rice wine vinegar

1 tbsp soy sauce

1 tbsp orange zest

1 tbsp canola oil

1 tbsp agave (see p. 250)

¼–½ tsp chili flakes, to taste

In a medium frying pan on high heat, bring 2 cups (500 mL) water and vinegar to a boil. Add tempeh, reduce heat to medium, cover, and cook for 5 minutes. Turn and cook for another 5 minutes. Remove from heat, discard cooking water, and refresh tempeh under cold water until cool to the touch.

Cut tempeh horizontally in half to get layers. Slice each layer into 9 uniform pieces.

In a small ziplock bag, combine all marinade ingredients. Add tempeh strips, toss to coat, then place in refrigerator to marinate for at least 1 hour, turning at least once.

Preheat barbecue to medium heat. Lay down a sheet of aluminum foil lightly brushed with oil and place tempeh strips on foil. Reserve marinade. Grill for 7–9 minutes on each side until golden, basting frequently with leftover marinade.

Sweet Chipotle Tempeh with Berry Glaze

I love, love, love tempeh made this way—it is sweet, spicy, fruity, more than a little sticky, and finger-licking good, either hot or cold. Great for an intimate backyard party.

MAKES 4 SERVINGS
Preparation time: 15 minutes + 1 hour marinating
Cooking time: 15 minutes

2 tsp apple cider vinegar
8 oz (230 g) tempeh, whole piece (see p. 252)

MARINADE
1 tbsp brown sugar
1 tbsp lime juice
1 tbsp soy sauce
1 tsp ground cumin
½–1 tsp chipotle powder, to taste (see p. 250)

BERRY GLAZE
2 tbsp agave (see p. 250)
2 tbsp vegan margarine
1 tbsp lime juice
1 cup (250 mL) fresh or thawed frozen blueberries

In a medium frying pan, bring 2 cups (500 mL) water and vinegar to a boil. Add tempeh, reduce heat to medium, cover pan, and cook for 5 minutes. Turn tempeh and cook for another 5 minutes. Remove from heat, discard cooking water, and refresh tempeh under cold water until cool to the touch.

Cut tempeh horizontally in half to get layers. Slice each layer into 6 equal (roughly ¾-in [2-cm] wide) strips.

In a small ziplock bag, combine all marinade ingredients. Add tempeh strips, toss to coat, then place in refrigerator to marinate for at least 1 hour, turning at least once.

Meanwhile, in a small bowl, cream together agave, margarine, and lime juice. Press berries through a medium sieve directly over bowl, using the back of a spoon. Discard seeds and skins (or save to use in a smoothie). Stir until combined well. If it doesn't emulsify, heat gently in microwave to slightly melt margarine, then stir again to combine well.

Preheat barbecue to medium heat. Lay down a sheet of aluminum foil lightly brushed with oil. Remove tempeh from marinade. Dip each slice into glaze before placing on foil. Reserve glaze. Grill tempeh for 7–9 minutes per side, brushing slices regularly with leftover glaze until it is all used up.

Seitan Skewers with Peach Salsa

Summertime, barbecues, and peaches: made for each other? These tasty skewers are a little sweet, easy to make, and perfect when paired with Peach Salsa. If it's not peach season, don't despair; make the skewers anyway and serve with another fruity salsa such as Melon & Corn (p. 75) or Cucumber & Kiwifruit (p. 77).

MAKES 4 SERVINGS

Preparation time: 10 minutes +
1 hour marinating

Cooking time: 10 minutes

¼ cup (60 mL) apple and peach juice combined, or apple juice only

2 tbsp lime juice

2 tbsp soy sauce

2 tbsp agave (see p. 250)

2 tsp sesame oil

1 tsp grated fresh ginger

1 tsp lime zest

1 garlic clove, minced

1 lb (500 g) seitan, your favorite kind, cut into ¾-in (2-cm) cubes (see p. 252)

¾ cup (375 mL) chopped red bell peppers

1 recipe Peach Salsa (p. 78)

In a large flat container with a resealable lid or in a large ziplock bag, combine juices, soy sauce, agave, oil, ginger, lime zest, and garlic. Add seitan, then place in refrigerator to marinate for at least 1 hour, turning after 30 minutes.

Meanwhile, soak skewers in water for 1 hour. Remove seitan from marinade and thread equal number of cubes, alternating with slices of red bell peppers, onto each skewer. Reserve marinade.

Preheat barbecue to medium heat. Lay down a sheet of aluminum foil lightly brushed with oil.

Grill skewers for 5 minutes each side, turning often, until seitan is browned. Baste frequently with left-over marinade.

You will need 8 8-in (20-cm) wooden skewers for this recipe.

Raspberry Balsamic-Glazed Seitan

Fresh berries for dessert are a summertime standard—so why not use them as part of the main course? This dish combines tender, barbecued seitan with fresh raspberries. Add a touch of chipotle chili powder to the glaze for a little kick.

MAKES 4 SERVINGS
Preparation time: 5 minutes
Cooking time: 10 minutes

2 tbsp agave (see p. 250)

2 tbsp vegan margarine

1 tbsp balsamic vinegar

1 garlic clove, minced

1 cup (250 mL) fresh or thawed frozen raspberries

1 lb (500 g) light "chicken-style" seitan (see p. 252)

In a small bowl, whisk together agave, margarine, vinegar, and garlic. If it doesn't emulsify, heat gently in microwave to slightly melt margarine, then stir again.

Press berries through a medium sieve directly into bowl with the back of a spoon. Discard seeds. Stir glaze mix until combined well.

Slice seitan into ½-in (1-cm) thick strips, then dip each strip into glaze. Reserve glaze.

Preheat barbecue to medium heat. Lay down a sheet of aluminum foil lightly brushed with oil. Place seitan on foil. Grill for about 5 minutes each side, until browned and sticky. Baste frequently with leftover glaze until it is all used up.

Mango Chutney Seitan Strips

Do you have jars of condiments in your refrigerator that you bought for a specific recipe and then never used again? This recipe came about when I needed to use up some mango chutney. It's a slightly spicy, fruity, creamy marinade that sticks to the seitan, creating a nice glaze once cooked.

MAKES 4 SERVINGS
Preparation time: *5 minutes +*
1 hour marinating
Cooking time: *15 minutes*

⅛ cup (80 mL) canned coconut milk

½ cup (125 mL) canned crushed pineapple in juice

3 tbsp mango chutney (see p. 251)

2 tbsp Thai sweet chili sauce (see p. 252)

1 tsp ground cumin

1 tsp Tandoori Spice Mix (p. 22)

½ tsp salt

¼ tsp chili flakes (optional)

salt, ground black pepper, and hot sauce to taste

1 lb (500 g) seitan, cut into ¼-in (6-mm) thick, 1-in (2.5-cm) wide strips (see p. 252)

In a blender, blend coconut milk, pineapple with its juices, mango chutney, chili sauce, cumin, Tandoori Spice Mix, salt, and chili flakes. Taste and season as desired.

Pour into a large flat container with a resealable lid or into a large ziplock bag. Add seitan strips and toss to coat. Place in refrigerator to marinate for at least 1 hour. Turn after 30 minutes.

Preheat barbecue to medium–medium-high heat. Lay down a sheet of aluminum foil lightly brushed with oil. Place seitan strips on foil. Reserve glaze. Grill for 5 minutes each side, until browned and sticky. Baste frequently with leftover glaze until it is all used up.

Seitan Satay with Spicy Peanut Sauce

When I lived in Thailand as an exchange student (many moons ago), I bought a peanut sauce like this from street vendors who sold it with hunks of toasted bread or satay sticks of mystery meat for dipping. I'm not so enthralled with mystery meat any more, but I still love the sauce, so I created a vegan satay to go along with it. Dip both the bread and seitan into the sauce.

MAKES 4–6 SERVINGS

Preparation time: 15 minutes + 1 hour marinating

Cooking time: 15 minutes

 (sauce only)

1 shallot, very finely chopped

1 tbsp grated fresh ginger

1 tbsp peanut or canola oil

¼ cup (60 mL) canned coconut milk

1½ tsp curry powder

¼ tsp ground turmeric

⅛–¼ tsp chili flakes, to taste

1 tbsp lemon juice

1½ tsp agave (see p. 250)

¼ tsp salt

1 lb (500 g) light "chicken style" seitan (see p. 252)

1 recipe Spicy Peanut Sauce (p. 71)

4 cups (1 L) Plain Rolls or Loaves (p. 186) or other firm white bread, cubed

In a large flat container with a resealable lid or in a large ziplock bag, combine shallots, ginger, oil, coconut milk, curry powder, turmeric, chili flakes, lemon juice, agave, and salt.

Slice seitan into 1-in (2.5-cm) thick strips. Add to marinade and toss to coat. Cover and marinate in refrigerator for at least 1 hour. Turn after 30 minutes.

Meanwhile, soak skewers in water for 1 hour.

Just before barbecuing, make Peanut Sauce so it's warm and ready to serve.

Remove seitan from marinade and thread 2–3 strips onto skewers (you will have some skewers left over). Brush or rub with remaining marinade.

Thread 6 or 7 cubes of bread onto each remaining skewer.

Preheat a lightly oiled barbecue to medium–medium-high heat. Grill skewers of bread for 4 minutes and skewers of seitan for 8–10. Turn as required to grill evenly, until golden.

You will need: 20 12-in (30-cm) wooden skewers for this recipe.

Spiced Oven Potato Wedges

What would grilled burgers be without a side of fries? These lightly spiced potato wedges are baked, not deep-fried, but they're addictive. Pre-cooking the spuds gives them light and fluffy insides.

MAKES 4 SERVINGS
Preparation time: 5 minutes
Cooking time: 45 minutes

4 medium Yukon Gold potatoes, 1¼–1½ lb (625 g–750 g), scrubbed or peeled as desired

2 tbsp olive oil

½ tsp salt, or to taste

¼ tsp smoked paprika

¼ tsp ground cumin

⅛ tsp ground turmeric

⅛ tsp pepper, or to taste

⅛ tsp chili flakes

salt and ground black pepper, to taste

Preheat oven to 425°F (220°C). Ready a large roasting dish and 2 clean tea towels.

Cut potatoes into wedge shapes no more than ½-inch (1-cm) thick.

In a large saucepan on high heat, cook potatoes in boiling water for 5 minutes to parboil. Drain well, then turn onto prepared tea towel, cover with second towel, and pat dry.

Pour oil into roasting dish and heat in oven for 2 minutes. Add potatoes, sprinkle with spices, and toss using a spatula (not your hands) to coat well.

Bake for 20 minutes, then turn and cook for another 20 minutes, until potatoes are golden and crisp. Taste and season as desired.

Feel free to adjust the spices—quantities and heat levels—to taste.

Grilled Zucchini Sticks

These zucchini sticks are a little lighter and healthier than the traditional ones encased in batter and deep-fried. The flavor of the zucchini really shines, enhanced by wine, mustard, and tarragon.

MAKES 2–4 SERVINGS

Preparation time: 5 minutes + 1 hour marinating

Cooking time: 15 minutes

2 tbsp white wine

1 garlic clove, minced

1 tsp mild grainy mustard

1 tsp agave (see p. 250)

1 tsp white wine vinegar

½ tsp salt

½ tsp dried tarragon

2 medium zucchinis, quartered lengthwise and cut into 3-in (8-cm) sticks

In a large flat container with resealable lid or in a large ziplock bag, combine wine, garlic, mustard, agave, vinegar, salt, and tarragon.

Add zucchini and toss to coat. Marinate for at least 1 hour, turning after 30 minutes. Reserve marinade.

Preheat barbecue to medium heat. Lay down a sheet of aluminum foil lightly brushed with oil. Grill zucchini for 5 minutes each side, until lightly browned, basting frequently with leftover marinade.

Smoky Barbecue Mushrooms

When marinated and grilled, these mushrooms are tender, sweet, and sour, with a hint of barbecue smokiness which accentuates their natural heartiness. I like my mushrooms really well done, but the cooking time in this recipe is for medium to well-done. Adjust cooking times to taste.

MAKES 4 SERVINGS

Preparation time: 5 minutes + 1 hour marinating
Cooking time: 10 minutes

3 tbsp grapeseed oil

3 tbsp maple syrup

2 tbsp soy sauce

2 tbsp brown sugar

1 tbsp pomegranate molasses (see p. 251)

1 tbsp tamarind paste (see p. 251)

1 tsp liquid smoke

1 tsp garlic powder

½ tsp smoked paprika

½ tsp ground ginger

¼ tsp ground fennel seeds

salt and ground black pepper, to taste

4 portobello mushrooms, caps only, sliced ½-in (1-cm) thick (remove gills if desired)

In a large flat container with a resealable lid or in a large ziplock bag, combine oil, syrup, soy sauce, sugar, pomegranate molasses, tamarind paste, liquid smoke, garlic powder, paprika, ginger, fennel seeds, salt, and pepper. Mix to combine well.

Add mushroom slices and toss to coat. Place in refrigerator and marinate for at least 1 hour. Turn after 30 minutes.

Preheat barbecue to medium heat. Lay down a sheet of aluminum foil lightly brushed with oil. Grill mushrooms for 8–10 minutes, until tender and browned.

Grilled Veggies

I love a starter (or even a light summer meal) of simply grilled vegetables served with Garlic Dipping Sauce (p. 55). Marinating the vegetables before grilling isn't absolutely necessary, but if you do so, you can use any of the marinades from this book. Place marinade ingredients in a large flat container with resealable lid or in a large ziplock bag, add the vegetables, and allow them to marinate (usually in the refrigerator) for at least 1 hour, turning after 30 minutes.

Corn

Peel off thick outside layers of husk, leaving softer light-green layers. Rub with a little oil, then wrap in aluminum foil.

Preheat grill to medium. Place corn on grill (away from direct heat), cover, and cook for 10 minutes. Turn and cook for another 10 minutes. Move corn over direct heat for final 5 minutes and turn frequently. The husk may be charred; remove it before serving.

Root and other hard vegetables (beets, carrots, parsnips, winter squash, etc.)

Cut vegetables into uniform pieces, either in slices, discs, or chunks. Season as desired.

Preheat grill to medium. Lay down a sheet of aluminum foil and place vegetables on foil over indirect heat to start. Cover and cook for 10 minutes. Turn and cook for another 10 minutes or more, until tender. Move vegetables onto direct heat for 5 minutes to char a little.

Other vegetables (bell peppers, asparagus, zucchini, onions, etc.)

Cut vegetables into uniform pieces, either in long strips or chunks. Leave asparagus spears whole. Season vegetables with a little salt, pepper, and/or herbs.

Preheat grill to medium. Lay down a sheet of aluminum foil and place vegetables on foil over direct heat. Cover and cook for 5 minutes. Turn vegetables and cook for another 5 minutes, or until cooked to your liking.

Garlic

Grilling garlic is basically the same method for roasting it in an oven: rub off outer paper-like layers of skin, then slice off very top of head, exposing tops of cloves. Preheat grill to medium. Place garlic on a sheet of aluminum foil, drizzle with a little oil, then wrap. Place on grill over indirect heat, cover, and cook 20–25 minutes, until soft and gooey.

YOU'D THINK I'D BE DONE
WITH *baking after having
written a whole book on the
subject, but the truth is, I love the
creativity I can bring to making
so many different kinds of baked
goods (and I love the end results,
of course!). The recipes in this
chapter focus on baked goods
both savory and sweet to serve
on Sunday morning brunch
picnics or get-togethers on your
patio. These items are also
transportable and adaptable for
out-of-doors, away-from-home
dining. Feel free to make your
own substitutions to taste: don't
like raspberries? Use blueberries.
Hate pecans, but love pistachios?
Swap them. Find ground ginger
overpowering? Leave it out. I'm
sure you'll find something here to
enhance and complete any
al fresco meal. Enjoy!*

baking
&
brunch

Nut & Seed Crackers

These slightly delicate crackers have a wonderful burst of "seedy" flavor over a subtly savory background. Especially good topped with rich pâtés or dips (see pp. 57–70 for ideas).

MAKES ABOUT 30 CRACKERS
Preparation time: 15 minutes
Cooking time: 10 minutes

1 cup (250 mL) all-purpose flour
½ cup (125 mL) ground almonds
1 tsp baking powder
¾ tsp salt
½ tsp ground black pepper
1 tbsp sesame seeds
1 tbsp poppy seeds
1 tbsp hemp seeds (see p. 251)
¼ cup (60 mL) canola oil
2 tbsp almond milk
3–5 tbsp vegetable stock

Preheat oven to 400°F (200°C). Line 2 large baking sheets with parchment paper.

In a large bowl, sift together flour, ground almonds, baking powder, salt, and pepper. Stir in seeds.

Make a well in center of dry ingredients. Add oil, milk, and stock and mix to form a stiff dough. If more liquid is required, add stock 1 tsp at a time until dough holds together when pressed.

Press dough into a ball. Turn out onto a lightly floured board and roll to about ⅛-in (3-mm) thick (as thin as you can). With a 2-in (5-cm) cookie cutter, cut out crackers. Place 1 in (2.5 cm) apart on prepared baking sheets. Re-roll scraps and cut out more crackers.

Bake for 8–10 minutes, until golden brown. Cool on sheets for 5 minutes, then transfer to a rack to complete cooling.

Store in a covered container.

Gluten-free Corn Crackers

These crackers utilize the wonderful flavor of masa harina, which I believe could be a crossover ingredient in a lot of dishes (you heard it from me first). I decided to go all out and make these gluten-free.

MAKES ABOUT 30 CRACKERS
Preparation time: *25 minutes*
Cooking time: *8 minutes*

2 tbsp olive oil

2 tbsp rice milk

1½ tsp ground chia seeds
   (see p. 250)

¼ cup (60 mL) fine cornmeal

¼ cup (60 mL) masa harina
   (see p. 251)

¼ cup (60 mL) yellow corn flour

¼ cup (60 mL) millet flour
   (see p. 251)

2 tbsp cornstarch

1 tsp dried oregano

½ tsp salt

½ tsp baking soda

¼ tsp ground black pepper

Preheat oven to 400°F (200°C). Line 2 large baking sheets with parchment paper.

In a large bowl, whisk together ¼ cup (60 mL) water, oil, rice milk, and chia seeds. Let sit for 10 minutes to thicken. Sift in cornmeal, masa harina, corn flour, millet flour, cornstarch, oregano, salt, baking soda, and pepper. Stir to combine. Mixture will look crumbly and a little dry. Knead dough until it holds together when pressed.

Roll dough out on a lightly floured board (use millet flour or yellow corn flour) to less than ⅛-in (3-mm) thick. With a 2-in (5-cm) cookie cutter, cut out crackers. With a spatula, place 1 in (2.5 cm) apart on prepared baking sheets. Re-roll scraps and cut out more crackers.

Bake for 8 minutes, until dry looking and firm to the touch.

Cool on trays for 5 minutes, then transfer to a rack to complete cooling.

Garlic Breadsticks

These are so good that my "garlic-phobic" children beg me to make them; they're perfect for munching at an outdoor party (beware the garlic breath!). If you're a bread (or garlic) lover, make a double batch, because they won't last long!

MAKES ABOUT 12 BREADSTICKS

Preparation time: 4 ½ hours, including rising time

Cooking time: 15 minutes

1 tsp sugar

1 tsp dried yeast

½ cup (125 mL) all-purpose flour

1 tbsp vital wheat gluten powder (see p. 252)

2 garlic cloves, minced

½ tsp garlic powder

½ tsp salt

½ cup (125 mL) all-purpose flour (for kneading)

1 tbsp oil (for coating bowl)

¼ cup (60 mL) your choice of flavorings: sesame seeds; poppy seeds; dried herbs; coarse salt; finely chopped mixed nuts (optional)

....

In a large bowl, combine ½ cup (125 mL) warm water, sugar, and yeast and let sit for 10 minutes to allow yeast to bubble. Stir in flour, gluten powder, garlic, garlic powder, and salt. Stir briskly 100 times. Let mixture sit for 15 minutes.

Stir in remaining flour and turn onto a floured board to knead. Flour may not be completely incorporated at first but will after a few minutes of kneading. Add more flour, 1 tbsp at a time, if dough is too sticky.

Knead vigorously for about 15 minutes, until dough is smooth and supple. (*Tip:* You can do this in 3-minute bursts; knead 3 minutes, rest 3 minutes, and repeat.) Form dough into a ball.

Coat large bowl with thin film of oil. Place dough in bowl and turn to coat completely in oil. Cover bowl and set in a warm place (such as a warm sunny corner of kitchen or inside a microwave oven) for about 1½ hours, until dough has doubled in size.

Punch dough down, knead for about 3 minutes, then return to bowl. Cover and return to warm place for second rise, about 1 hour, until dough has doubled in size again.

Remove dough from bowl and knead lightly. Shape into 12 1-tbsp sized balls. Roll each ball in flavoring of your choice, or leave them plain.

Shape into breadsticks about 15 in (38 cm) long and ¼ in (6 mm) in diameter by rolling on floured board or between hands.

Preheat oven to 400°F (200°C). Place breadsticks on baking sheets and let them rest while oven heats.

Bake for 12–15 minutes, until golden brown and crisp.

Plain Rolls or Loaves

This basic recipe makes lovely soft rolls or loaves. You can easily jazz it up by adding additional ingredients (such as finely chopped nuts or seeds, or fresh or dried herbs) with the first addition of flour.

MAKES 1 9-IN (2-L) LOAF OR 12 ROLLS

Preparation time: 3½ hours, including time for rising

Cooking time: 25 minutes

¼ cup (60 mL) plain soy milk

2 tsp dried yeast

1 tsp sugar

2 cups (500 mL) white bread flour or 2 cups (500 mL) all-purpose flour + 2 tbsp vital wheat gluten powder (see p. 252)

¼ cup (60 mL) wheat germ

1 tbsp lemon juice

1 tbsp canola oil

1 tsp salt

1 cup (250 mL) white bread flour or 1 cup (250 mL) all-purpose flour + 1 tbsp vital wheat gluten powder (for kneading)

1 tbsp oil (for coating bowl)

....

In a large bowl, combine 1 cup (250 mL) warm water, milk, yeast, and sugar and let sit for 10 minutes to allow yeast to bubble. Stir in 2 cups (500 mL) flour, wheat germ, lemon juice, oil, and salt. Stir briskly 100 times. Let mixture sit for 15 minutes.

Stir in remainder of flour and turn onto floured board to knead. Flour may not be completely incorporated at first but will after a few minutes of kneading. Add more flour, 1 tbsp at a time, if dough is too sticky.

Knead vigorously for about 15 minutes, until dough is smooth and supple. (*Tip:* You can do this in 3-minute bursts; knead 3 minutes, rest 3 minutes, and repeat.) Form dough into a ball.

Coat large bowl with thin film of oil. Place dough in bowl and turn to coat completely in oil. Cover bowl and set in a warm place (such as a warm sunny corner of kitchen or inside a microwave oven) for 1½ hours, until dough has doubled in size.

Punch dough down, knead for about 3 minutes, then return to bowl. Cover and return to warm place for second rise, about 1 hour, until dough has doubled in size again.

Remove dough from bowl. On lightly floured surface, knead lightly for 2–3 minutes. Shape into 12 uniform rolls or 1 large log shape.

Place on a lightly oiled medium baking sheet (for rolls) or in lightly oiled 9-in (2-L) loaf pan. Cover and let sit for 30 minutes, and allow to rise again.

Preheat oven to 400°F (200°C) while dough rises, about 30 minutes. Brush top(s) with soy milk or oil if desired.

Bake for 20–25 minutes for buns or 35–40 minutes for a loaf, until bread is golden brown. To test loaf for doneness, remove from pan (careful, it will be hot!) and lightly tap bottom of loaf; it should sound hollow.

Allow to cool completely on a rack before slicing.

Corn & Olive Focaccia

You can serve this soft and delicious bread at a backyard barbecue or have it for an al fresco breakfast—or any time. The corn (in all its forms) adds a lovely hint of flavor and texture that complements the salty olives. This recipe uses that masa harina you may have in the cupboard after making Slow Cooker Tomatillo & Tomato Tamales (p. 43).

MAKES I 8-IN (20-CM) SQUARE LOAF, ABOUT 8 SERVINGS

Preparation time: *2½ hours, including rising time*

Cooking time: *25 minutes*

2 tsp dry yeast

1 tbsp sugar

1 cup (250 mL) all-purpose flour

¼ cup (60 mL) fine cornmeal

¼ cup (60 mL) masa harina (see p. 251)

¼ cup (60 mL) chopped black olives

¼ cup (60 mL) corn kernels, fresh, or if canned, then drain and rinse, or frozen and thawed

1 tbsp olive oil

1 tsp salt

1¾ cup (415 mL) white bread flour, or 1¾ cup (415 mL) all-purpose flour + 2 tbsp vital wheat gluten powder (for kneading) (see p. 252)

1 tbsp olive oil (for coating bowl)

¼ cup halved black olives, to garnish (optional)

....

In a large bowl, combine 1½ cups (375 mL) warm water, yeast, and sugar. Let sit for 10 minutes to allow yeast to bubble. Add flour, cornmeal, masa harina, olives, corn, oil, and salt. Stir well to combine and let sit for 30 minutes.

Stir in remainder of flour and turn onto a clean floured board. Knead vigorously for about 15 minutes, until dough is smooth and supple. (*Tip:* You can do this in 3-minute bursts; knead 3 minutes, rest 3 minutes, and repeat.) Form dough into a ball.

Coat large bowl with thin film of oil. Place dough in bowl and turn to coat completely in oil. Cover bowl and set in a warm place (such as a warm sunny corner of kitchen or inside a microwave oven) for 1¼ hours, until dough has doubled in size.

Lightly oil an 8-in (20-cm) square brownie or cake pan.

Punch dough down, knead for about 3 minutes, then return to bowl. Cover and return to warm place for second rise, about 30–45 minutes, until dough has doubled in size again.

Preheat oven to 375°F (190°C) while dough rises for another 30 minutes.

Make deep thumb indents about 1-in (2.5-cm) apart in top of dough. Place ½ black olive in each. Brush top of dough with oil.

Bake for 25 minutes, until golden brown.

Cool in pan for 5 minutes, then transfer to a rack to complete cooling.

Buckwheat & Onion Mini-Loaves

I use raw buckwheat in this recipe, but if you prefer it toasted (also called kasha), feel free to use it. These little loaves are good both hot out of the oven or cool. Serve for brunch or lunch with a salad.

MAKES 8 MINI-LOAVES OR 12 MUFFINS
Preparation time: 25 minutes
Cooking time: 25 minutes

1 cup (250 mL) water
½ cup (125 mL) uncooked raw buckwheat, rinsed (see p. 250)
1 tbsp olive oil
1½ cups (375 mL) quartered and thinly sliced onions
1 tbsp light brown sugar
2 cups (500 mL) all-purpose flour
2 tsp baking powder
½ tsp baking soda
½ tsp ground black pepper
1¼ tsp salt
1½ cups (375 mL) plain soy milk
2 tbsp olive oil
2 tbsp canola oil

....

In a small saucepan on high heat, bring water to a boil. Add buckwheat, cover pan, and reduce heat to low. Simmer for 15–20 minutes, until liquid is absorbed and buckwheat is tender.

Once cooked, spread buckwheat on a large plate and let cool for 10 minutes, to room temperature.

In a large frying pan on medium, heat 1 tbsp oil. Sauté onions for 7–10 minutes, until soft and golden. Add brown sugar and cook for another 5 minutes to lightly caramelize. Add a splash of water if it sticks. Volume will reduce by about half. Remove from heat and let cool for 15 minutes.

Preheat oven to 375°F (190°C). Spray mini-loaf pan with non-stick spray.

In a large bowl, sift together flour, baking power, baking soda, pepper, and salt. Make a well in center of dry ingredients and add soy milk, olive oil, canola oil, cooked buckwheat, and onions. Fold wet ingredients into dry to just combine.

Spoon mixture evenly into pan. Bake for 25–30 minutes, until tops are lightly browned and a toothpick inserted in the center of a loaf comes out clean.

Cool 5 minutes in pan, then transfer to a rack to complete cooling.

A mini-loaf pan is like a muffin pan, but it has 8 rectangular slots instead of the usual 12 circular ones. You can also use a regular muffin pan.

Muffins of the Americas

The ingredients for these goodness-packed muffins (great for the hiking trail) come from two continents, North and South American. Even my quinoa-hating husband ate three and pronounced them delicious!

MAKES 12 MUFFINS
Preparation time: 20 minutes
Cooking time: 20–25 minutes

TOPPING

1 tbsp finely chopped dried cranberries

1 tbsp chopped sunflower seeds

1 tbsp chopped pumpkin seeds

1 tbsp finely chopped Brazil nuts

1 tbsp finely chopped pecans

¼ cup (60 mL) fine breadcrumbs or panko

1 tsp sunflower or canola oil

MUFFINS

1¾ cups (415 mL) almond milk

¼ cup (60 mL) canola oil

1 tsp lime juice

1 cup (250 mL) cooked and cooled quinoa

2 tbsp finely chopped cilantro

2 tbsp finely chopped red onions

2 tbsp corn kernels, fresh, or if canned then drain and rinse, or frozen and thawed

2 tbsp finely chopped red bell peppers

1½ cups (375 mL) all-purpose flour

⅓ cup (80 mL) quinoa flour (see p. 251)

⅓ cup (80 mL) yellow corn flour

2 tsp baking powder

1 tsp baking soda

1 tsp salt

In a small bowl, toss all topping ingredients together. Set aside.

Preheat oven to 375°F (190°C). Spray muffin pan with non-stick spray.

In a large bowl, combine almond milk, oil, and lime juice. Let sit 2–3 minutes to thicken. Stir in cooked quinoa, cilantro, onions, corn, and bell peppers, and mix to combine well. Sift in flour, baking powder, baking soda, and salt. Stir to just combine. Spoon mixture into prepared muffin pan.

Top each muffin with 2 tsp topping mix. Stir gently to incorporate a little into tops of muffins. Bake for 20–25 minutes, until a toothpick inserted in the center of a muffin comes out clean.

Cool in pan for 5 minutes, then transfer to a rack to complete cooling.

Savory Sausage Muffins

A little bit Aussie Sausage Roll, a little bit English Toad in the Hole, and a little bit Canadian Tim Horton's Breakfast Sandwich, this is a muffin version of a favorite breakfast or brunch food. Some people like them with ketchup on the side to dip…

MAKES 12 MUFFINS
Preparation time: 10 minutes
Cooking time: 25 minutes

2 cups (500 mL) + 3 tbsp plain soy milk

2 tbsp lemon juice

¼ cup (60 mL) canola oil

1¼ cups (310 mL) all-purpose flour

1 cup (250 mL) whole wheat pastry flour

¼ cup (60 mL) quinoa or millet flour (see p. 251)

¼ cup (60 mL) cornstarch

3 tbsp nutritional yeast (see p. 251)

3 tsp baking powder

1 tsp baking soda

1 tsp salt

¼ tsp ground black pepper

¼ tsp onion powder

¼ tsp garlic powder

¼ tsp ground dry mustard

¾ (185 mL)–1 cup (250 mL) vegan sausage, cut into ¼-in (6-mm) cubes (try Garlic & Sage Sausages, p. 160)

3 spring onions, finely chopped

Preheat oven to 375°F (190°C). Spray muffin pan with non-stick spray.

In a large bowl, whisk together milk, juice, and oil. Sift in flours, cornstarch, nutritional yeast, baking powder, baking soda, salt, pepper, onion powder, garlic powder, and dry mustard, and mix until just combined. Stir in sausage and spring onions. Spoon batter into prepared muffin pan.

Bake about 25 minutes, until a toothpick inserted in the center of a muffin comes out clean.

Cool for 5 minutes in pan, then transfer to a rack to complete cooling.

Teff Biscuits

Ever so slightly accented with lemon, these tender gluten-free biscuits pair well with salads such as the Quinoa & Avocado 'Slaw (p. 131) or items off the grill, such as the Mango Chutney Seitan Strips (p. 172).

MAKES ABOUT 12 BISCUITS
Preparation time: 20 minutes
Cooking time: 12 minutes

1 cup (250 mL) plain soy milk

2 tsp ground chia seeds
(see p. 250)

1 tbsp lemon juice

1 tsp lemon zest (optional)

1 cup (250 mL) teff flour
(see p. 251)

¾ cup (185 mL) millet flour
(see p. 251)

2 tbsp cornstarch

2 tsp baking powder

1 tsp lemon pepper

½ tsp salt

2 tbsp vegan margarine

2 tbsp vegan shortening

2 tbsp cold coconut oil

Preheat oven to 425°F (220°C). Line a large baking sheet with parchment paper.

In a small bowl, whisk together milk, chia seeds, lemon juice, and lemon zest. Let thicken for 10 minutes.

In a large bowl, sift together flour, cornstarch, baking powder, lemon pepper, and salt. Cut margarine, shortening, and oil into flour mixture with a pastry cutter or two knives held together, until mixture resembles breadcrumbs. Stir in soured milk to form a thick, soft, wet dough.

Turn dough onto a lightly floured surface. Stretch and press dough to form a circle 1-in (2.5-cm) in height.

With a 2-in (5-cm) circular cookie cutter, cut out biscuits. Gently re-form dough scraps and cut biscuits until dough is used up.

With a spatula, place 2 in (5 cm) apart on prepared baking sheet. Bake for about 12 minutes, until biscuits have risen and bottoms are lightly browned.

Teff is the tiny grain of a native North African grass that you may know as an ingredient in the Ethiopian flatbread *injera*. It is naturally gluten-free and a good source of iron, calcium, protein, and fiber. You can buy teff flour at health food stores or Ethiopian markets.

Savory Sausage Muffins (p. 191)

Teff Biscuits (opposite)

Muffins of the Americas (p. 190)

Triple Chocolate Waffles

Rich, decadent, but not overly sweet, these waffles will satisfy your early- morning chocolate requirements.

MAKES 4 WAFFLES

Preparation time: 10 minutes

Cooking time: about 15 minutes

¾ cup (185 mL) semi-sweet vegan chocolate chips

½ cup (125 mL) maple syrup

3 tbsp canola oil

1 tsp vanilla extract

1¼ cups (310 mL) chocolate soy milk

1¾ cups (415 mL) all-purpose flour

3 tbsp cocoa powder

2 tsp baking powder

½ tsp salt

Heat waffle iron, according to instructions. Make sure it's ready to use as soon as batter is mixed.

In a large bowl, combine chocolate chips, syrup, oil, and vanilla. Place bowl in microwave oven on high, and in 3 or 4 20-second intervals, melt, stirring well after each heating.

Whisk in milk and combine well, until smooth. Sift in flour, cocoa powder, baking powder, and salt and mix to just combine.

Spray plates of waffle iron with non-stick spray before making each waffle.

With a heat-proof spatula, spread batter on iron (batter will be thick). Cook according to instructions.

Banana Spelt Waffles

A healthy waffle made without oil (there's enough moisture from the banana and coconut milk). These are nice for a weekend brunch on the patio. Serve with a little vegan margarine spread on top and drizzled with maple syrup.

MAKES 4 WAFFLES
Preparation time: *10 minutes*
Cooking time: *about 15 minutes*

2 very ripe bananas
½ cup (125 mL) canned coconut
  milk thinned with ½ cup
  (125 mL) water
¼ cup (60 mL) sugar
1 tsp vanilla extract
¼ tsp banana or vanilla extract
1½ cups (375 mL) spelt flour
  (see p. 251)
1½ tsp baking powder
½ tsp pumpkin pie spice

In a large bowl, mash bananas thoroughly; they should be almost liquid. Whisk in coconut milk, sugar, and extracts.

Sift in flour, baking powder, and spices and mix until just combined. Set aside.

Heat waffle iron according to instructions. Spray plates of waffle iron with non-stick spray before making each waffle. Cook according to directions.

Nutty Banana Spelt Waffles
For added crunch and flavor, add 2 tbsp finely chopped pecans (or other nut of choice) to batter when adding flour.

Quinoa & Pineapple Muffins

The flavors of quinoa and pineapple—nutty grains and sweet fruit—seem to work really well together in these golden-hued muffins.

MAKES 12 MUFFINS
Preparation time: 10 minutes
Cooking time: 20–25 minutes

1¼ cups (310 mL) all-purpose flour
¾ cup (185 mL) whole wheat pastry flour
½ cup (125 mL) quinoa flour (see p. 251)
2½ tsp baking powder
1 tsp baking soda
½ tsp salt
⅛ tsp ground nutmeg
¾ cup (185 mL) rice milk
½ cup (125 mL) cooked quinoa
1¼ cup (310 mL) crushed canned pineapple with juices
⅔ cup (160 mL) sugar
½ tsp vanilla extract
¼ cup (60 mL) canola oil

Preheat oven to 375°F (190°C). Spray muffin pan with non-stick spray.

In a large bowl, sift together flours, baking powder, baking soda, salt, and nutmeg.

In another large bowl, combine milk, quinoa, pineapple with juices, sugar, vanilla, and oil. Mix to combine well. Add liquid ingredients to dry and mix to just combine. Spoon batter into muffin pan.

Bake for 20–25 minutes until a toothpick inserted into the center of a muffin comes out clean.

Cool for 5 minutes in pan, then transfer to a rack to complete cooling.

Strawberry & Basil Scones

The best time to make these is at the height of summer, when your local farmer's market or fruit and vegetable stand is bursting with ripe strawberries and huge bunches of basil. Serve with sliced fresh strawberries or touched up with a little vegan margarine. Good warm out of the oven or cool.

MAKES 10 SCONES
Preparation time: 15 minutes
Cooking time: 15 minutes

1 cup (250 mL) plain soy milk

1 tsp apple cider vinegar

3 tbsp strawberry jam

3 tbsp sugar

3 tbsp canola oil

1 tsp strawberry or vanilla extract

2 cups (500 mL) all-purpose flour

1 cup (250 mL) whole wheat pastry flour

3½ tsp baking powder

1 tsp baking soda

½ tsp salt

½ cup (125 mL) finely diced fresh strawberries, about 8 medium

2 heaping tbsp finely chopped fresh basil

Preheat oven to 375°F (190°C). Line a baking sheet with parchment paper.

In a large bowl, combine soy milk and vinegar. Let thicken for 5 minutes. Stir in jam, sugar, oil, and extract, and whisk to combine and eliminate large lumps of jam.

Sift in flours, baking powder, baking soda, and salt. Mix to just combine. Gently fold in strawberries and basil.

Portion dough into 10 scones with a ⅓-cup (80-mL) measure. Place on baking sheet and bake for 15–20 minutes, until lightly browned.

Cool on baking sheet for 5 minutes, then transfer to a rack to complete cooling, or serve warm.

Baklava Scones

These scones are based on the Mediterranean (mainly Greek and Turkish) dessert that's loaded with nuts and wrapped in phyllo pastry. The original baklava is sweet and sticky with loads of honey. This version is honey-free and nowhere near as sweet (or sticky), but every bit as delicious.

MAKES 12 SCONES
Preparation time: 15 minutes
Cooking time: 15 minutes

1½ cups (375 mL) almond milk

1 tbsp lemon juice

3¾ cups (890 mL) all-purpose flour

½ cup (125 mL) ground walnuts

½ cup (125 mL) finely chopped pistachio nuts

2 tsp baking powder

½ tsp baking soda

½ tsp salt

¼ tsp ground cardamom

1 tbsp rose water or 1 tbsp water with 3 drops rose extract (see p. 252)

⅓ cup (80 mL) agave (see p. 250)

¼ cup (60 mL) packed light brown sugar

¼ cup (60 mL) canola oil

¼ cup (60 mL) roughly chopped pistachios

2 tbsp agave

Preheat oven to 375°F (190°C). Line a large baking sheet with parchment paper.

In a medium bowl, combine almond milk and lemon juice. Let sit for 5 minutes to thicken.

In a large bowl, whisk together flour, nuts, baking powder, baking soda, salt, and cardamom. Stir in rose water, agave, sugar, and oil and mix to combine well. Stir in soured milk and mix to just combine.

Divide mixture into 12 equal portions. Shape into triangles (if possible; mixture is sticky, so just do your best) and place on baking sheet. Gently press 1 tbsp chopped pistachios into top of each scone. Bake for 15–18 minutes, until lightly golden.

Cool on sheet for 5 minutes then transfer, along with parchment paper, to a rack to complete cooling.

While still warm, drizzle each scone with agave.

Before baking, the batter is very moist, but there's no need to add extra flour.

Loaded Banana Bread

My younger daughter loves banana bread with chocolate chips, so this recipe is especially for her. It's loaded with chocolate chips—so many that you can't cut it without getting the knife all chocolate-y.

MAKES 1 9 X 5-IN (2-L) LOAF (ABOUT 8 SERVINGS)
Preparation time: *10 minutes*
Cooking time: *50–55 minutes*

3 very ripe medium bananas

¼ cup (60 mL) plain soy milk

¼ cup (60 mL) canola oil

¼ cup (60 mL) brown rice syrup (see p. 250)

1 tsp vanilla extract

½ tsp banana or vanilla extract

1¾ cups (415 mL) all-purpose flour

2 tbsp cornstarch

2 tsp baking powder

½ tsp salt

½ tsp ground cinnamon

½ tsp baking soda

¾–1 cup (185–250 mL) vegan chocolate chips

Preheat oven to 350°F (180°C). Line a 9 x 5-in (2-L) loaf pan with parchment paper.

In a large bowl, mash bananas until smooth and creamy. Add soy milk, oil, syrup, and extracts and whisk until combined well. Sift in flour, cornstarch, baking powder, salt, cinnamon, and baking soda and mix to just combine. Stir in chocolate chips.

Pour batter into prepared loaf pan and smooth top. Bake for 50–55 minutes, until a toothpick inserted in the center comes out clean. If there's chocolate on toothpick, ignore it; test doneness of batter. If top browns too quickly, cover pan with sheet of parchment paper and continue to bake.

Cool loaf for 10 minutes in pan, then transfer to a rack to complete cooling.

FRESH FRUIT IS AN IDEAL SUMMERTIME *dessert; many types—berries, melons, and stone fruits like peaches and nectarines— are perfectly ripe and in season, and they're both easy to transport and to eat once you get to your destination. But this chapter gives you options for more traditional sweet finishes, from simple cakes to pies, while keeping in mind that the desserts need to be able to travel well and be eaten with minimal plates and cutlery.*

I don't recommend that you pack ice cream in your picnic hamper or even in a cooler to take to a barbecue. But this chapter would be incomplete without some recipes for everyone's favorite summer dessert, which you can serve at backyard parties. These soft ice creams are all delectably smooth and rich. Because of the oil in the recipes, an ice cream machine won't freeze the mixture completely but will aerate it nicely and cool it to the point where only small ice crystals will be formed, keeping the texture luscious. If you don't have an ice cream machine, never fear; you can still make the ice cream recipes using the method outlined on p. 204.

desserts

Making ice cream without an ice cream maker

This method is more time-consuming than with an ice cream maker, and the results may not be as smooth, but they'll be every bit as luscious.

1. Mix base according to instructions that follow, and chill according to recipe.
2. Once chilled, transfer to large shallow container (8 x 12-in [20 x 25-cm] is ideal) and place on a flat surface in freezer. Freeze for 45 minutes, until just firm and frozen at edges.
3. With a fork or handheld blender, vigorously mix ice cream for at least 2–3 minutes, until thoroughly mixed and smooth.
4. Return to freezer and freeze for another 30–45 minutes.
5. Repeat stirring and freezing process for 3–4 hours, until mixture is totally frozen but remains smooth and as ice crystal-free as possible (some crystals will form naturally).
6. Transfer to a freezer-safe, airtight container and store in freezer for up to 1 week.

Ice Cream Cookies

Use ice cream from any of the recipes that follow to sandwich together two large cookies (flat sides facing), then place on a baking sheet in freezer. (I particularly enjoy using Chai Tea Cookies (p. 230) or Espresso Cookies (p. 231) with Vanilla (p. 206) or Chocolate (p. 209) ice cream.) When frozen solid (check after 2 hours), wrap individually in cling film and store in freezer.

Vanilla Ice Cream (p. 206)
with Cherry Pie Filling (p. 215)

Vanilla Ice Cream

My children love vanilla ice cream above all others, with one exception (see opposite). This is a weekend treat for them all summer; they often request it in the middle of winter too!

MAKES 4 CUPS (1 L)

Preparation time: about 15 minutes + 8 hours chilling + 30 minutes processing + at least 2 hours freezing

S

6-oz (175-g) firm silken tofu
¾ cup (185 mL) icing (confectioner's) sugar
¾ cup (185 mL) sugar
¾ cup (185 mL) canola oil
1½ cups (375 mL) plain soy milk
1 tbsp vanilla extract
1 tsp white balsamic vinegar (see p. 252)

In a blender, combine all ingredients. Start at a slow speed, then increase speed and blend until mixture is completely smooth and thick. Stop to scrape sides of blender as required.

Transfer blender jar to refrigerator to chill for 8 hours or overnight.

In an ice cream machine, process mixture for 30 minutes, or according to machine instructions, until aerated and cooled.

○ Add scrapings from a vanilla bean and reduce vanilla extract to 1 tsp.

Mint Chocolate Chip Ice Cream

This is the only ice cream my children request, other than vanilla. It's especially good if made into ice cream sandwiches with Nut & Seed Gluten-free Cookies (p. 235).

MAKES 4 CUPS (I L)

Preparation time: about 15 minutes + 8 hours chilling + 30 minutes processing + at least 2 hours freezing

S

6 oz (175 g) firm silken tofu

¾ cup (185 mL) icing (confectioner's) sugar

¾ cup (185 mL) sugar

¾ cup (185 mL) canola oil

¾ cup (185 mL) plain soy milk

¾ cup (185 mL) soy cream

¼ tsp vanilla extract

¾ tsp mint extract

1 tsp white balsamic vinegar (see p. 252)

1 drop green food coloring (optional)

¾ cup (185 mL) vegan chocolate mini-chips

In a blender, combine tofu, sugars, oil, soy milk and cream, vanilla, mint extract, vinegar, and food coloring. Start at a slow speed, then increase speed and blend until mixture is completely smooth and thick. Stop to scrape sides of blender as required.

Transfer blender jar to refrigerator to chill overnight.

In an ice cream machine, process mixture for 30 minutes, or according to machine instructions, until aerated and cooled. Stir in chocolate chips.

Mocha Almond Ice Cream

Packed with toasted almonds, hints of coffee, and rich chocolate, this indulgent ice cream is a perfect after-dinner treat to serve while sitting on the deck with your loved ones, watching the sun go down.

MAKES 4 CUPS (1 L)

Preparation time: about 15 minutes + 8 hours chilling + 30 minutes processing + at least 2 hours freezing

½ cup (125 mL) canola oil

¾ cup (185 mL) vegan chocolate chips

6-oz (175-g) firm silken tofu

1 cup (250 mL) icing (confectioner's) sugar

1 cup (250 mL) sugar

1½ tbsp instant coffee granules

1½ cups (375 mL) chocolate, soy, or almond milk

1 tsp vanilla extract

¼ tsp almond extract

1 tsp white balsamic vinegar (see p. 252)

½ cup (125 mL) roughly chopped, toasted, salted almonds

In a medium saucepan on medium heat, melt oil and chocolate chips. Stir until smooth.

In a blender, combine tofu, sugars, coffee granules, milk, vanilla, almond extract, and vinegar. Start at a slow speed, then increase speed and blend until mixture is completely smooth and thick. Stop to scrape sides of blender as required. Add oil and chocolate mixture to blender and blend until thoroughly mixed and smooth.

Transfer blender jar to refrigerator to chill overnight.

In ice cream machine, process mixture for 30 minutes, or according to machine instructions, until aerated and cooled. Stir in almonds to distribute evenly.

Triple Chocolate Ice Cream

My friend Jessie has been going gaga for this ice cream ever since I first made it for her when she was pregnant and had chocolate cravings. It's for all of you chocolate monsters out there!

MAKES 4 CUPS (1 L)

Preparation time: about 15 minutes + 8 hours chilling + 30 minutes processing + at least 2 hours freezing

½ cup (125 mL) canola oil

¾ cup (185 mL) vegan chocolate chips

6-oz (175-g) firm silken tofu

1 cup (250 mL) icing (confectioner's) sugar

1 cup (250 mL) sugar

2 tbsp Dutch processed cocoa powder

1½ cups (375 mL) chocolate soy milk

1 tsp vanilla extract

1 tsp white balsamic vinegar (see p. 252)

½ cup (125 mL) vegan chocolate chips (optional)

In a medium saucepan on medium heat, melt oil and chocolate chips. Stir until smooth.

In a blender, combine tofu, sugars, cocoa powder, soy milk, vanilla, and vinegar. Start at a slow speed, then increase speed and blend until mixture is completely smooth and thick. Stop to scrape sides of blender as required. Add oil and chocolate mixture to blender and blend until thoroughly mixed and smooth.

Transfer blender jar to refrigerator to chill overnight.

In an ice cream machine, process mixture for 30 minutes, or according to machine instructions, until aerated and cooled.

Stir ½ cup (125 mL) vegan chocolate chips into mixture before freezing.

Coconut Ice Cream

This ice cream always leaves me wanting "just a little bit more." Rich and creamy and nicely textured with added coconut, this is a delicious way to cool down on a summer's day.

MAKES 4 CUPS (1 L)

Preparation time: about 15 minutes + 8 hours chilling + 30 minutes processing + at least 2 hours freezing

2 14-oz (398-mL) can full-fat coconut milk

3 tbsp melted coconut oil

¾ cup (185 mL) sugar

¾ cup (185 mL) icing (confectioner's) sugar

2 tbsp arrowroot powder (see p. 250)

½ tsp coconut extract (optional)

½ cup (125 mL) unsweetened shredded coconut (optional, or toast before adding)

Place 1 can of coconut milk in refrigerator overnight. Open can—do not shake—and scoop off ½ cup cream from surface.

In a blender, process coconut cream with contents of second can of coconut milk, melted oil, sugars, arrowroot, and extract until creamy and smooth.

Transfer blender jar to refrigerator to chill overnight. Stir in shredded coconut and mix to distribute evenly.

In an ice cream machine, process mixture for 30 minutes, or according to machine instructions, until aerated and cooled.

Banana & Carrot Cake

Moist, like all good carrot cakes should be, with a subtle banana flavor, this is one cake you'll want to have at your picnic. Dress it up as much as you like, as occasion demands. If eating close to home, I like to ice it as a 2-layer cake, but if transporting, I usually leave it as a single layer and dust it with icing sugar.

MAKES 2 SINGLE-LAYER CAKES OR 1 TWO-LAYER CAKE, ABOUT 10–12 SERVINGS

Preparation time: 20 minutes
Cooking time: 25–30 minutes

2 very ripe large bananas

1 cup (250 mL) sugar

¾ cup (185 mL) rice milk

½ cup (125 mL) canned coconut milk

¼ cup (60 mL) unsweetened applesauce

2 tbsp softened coconut oil

1 tsp vanilla extract

1⅓ packed cups (330 mL) finely grated carrots

2 cups (500 mL) all-purpose flour

2 tsp baking powder

1 tsp baking soda

1 tsp salt

1 tsp ground cinnamon

¼ tsp ground nutmeg

¼ tsp ground cardamom

Preheat oven to 375°F (190°C) and line 2 9-in (23-cm) square cake pans with parchment paper.

In a large bowl, mash bananas until very smooth. Stir in sugar, rice milk, coconut milk, applesauce, oil, and vanilla, and whisk to combine well. Stir in carrots and mix well to evenly distribute.

Sift in flour, baking powder, baking soda, salt, cinnamon, nutmeg, and cardamom and stir until no large lumps remain.

Pour into prepared cake pans and smooth tops. Bake for 25–30 minutes, until sides have pulled away from pan, top springs back when gently pressed, and a toothpick inserted in center comes out clean.

Cool in pans for 5 minutes, then transfer to a rack to complete cooling.

Hazelnut Latte Cupcakes

You know those hazelnut lattes you buy at the coffee shop that are really dessert in a cup masquerading as a beverage? Here's that drink as a cupcake, complete with sprinkled sugar topping.

MAKES 12 CUPCAKES
Preparation time: 10 minutes
Cooking time: 20–22 minutes

1 cup (250 mL) plain soy milk
½ cup (125 mL) + 2 tbsp hazelnut-flavored coffee syrup
¼ cup (60 mL) canola oil
3 heaping tbsp light brown sugar, packed
1¼ tsp vanilla extract
¼ tsp almond extract
¼ cup (60 mL) ground toasted hazelnuts
2 cups (500 mL) all-purpose flour
2 tsp baking powder
½ tsp baking soda
½ tsp salt
2 tbsp instant coffee powder or granules
¼ cup (60 mL) icing (confectioner's) sugar

Preheat oven to 375°F (190°C). Line a muffin pan with cupcake liners.

In a large bowl, combine soy milk, syrup, oil, brown sugar, and extracts. Mix well to combine. Sift in ground nuts, flour, baking powder, baking soda, salt, and instant coffee and mix to just combine.

Spoon mixture into muffin pan. Bake for 20–22 minutes, until a toothpick inserted in the center of a muffin comes out clean.

Allow cupcakes to cool in pan for 5 minutes, then transfer to a rack to complete cooling. Once completely cool, with a sieve, dust with icing sugar.

If your supermarket doesn't sell flavored syrups for coffee, a local coffee shop may. They may even sell you just the amount you need, so you don't have to buy a whole bottle.

Hazelnut Mocha Latte Cupcakes
Replace 2 tbsp flour with cocoa powder.

Almond Latte Cupcakes
Replace ground hazelnuts and hazelnut syrup with ground almonds and almond-flavored syrup.

Apricot Bundt Cake

This cake is based on the recipe for Malva Pudding, a very sweet Cape Dutch hot dessert. I veganized it, made it to serve cold, and reduced the sweetness.

MAKES 10–12 SERVINGS
Preparation time: *15 minutes*
Cooking time: *40–45 minutes*

2 cups (500 mL) plain soy milk
2 tsp apple cider vinegar
⅓ cup (80 mL) vegan margarine, room temperature
⅔ cup (160 mL) sugar
¼ cup (60 mL) apricot jam
2 tsp vanilla extract
3 cups (750 mL) all-purpose flour
4 tsp baking powder
1 tsp salt
½ cup (125 mL) finely chopped dried apricots
2 tbsp icing (confectioner's) sugar (optional)

Preheat oven to 350°F (180°C). Oil a 10-in (25-cm) Bundt pan with margarine or shortening.

In a small bowl, combine soy milk and vinegar. Let sit for 5 minutes to thicken.

In a large bowl, cream together margarine and sugar for 3–4 minutes until light and fluffy. Stir in jam and vanilla and mix to combine well for 2–3 minutes, so that no large lumps of jam remain. Stir in soy milk mixture and mix well. (It may look curdled at this point; don't worry.)

Sift in flour, baking powder, and salt. Stir in apricots and mix to combine well. Carefully pour batter into prepared pan, then smooth top.

Bake for 40–45 minutes, until cake has risen, is golden, pulls away from sides of pan and a toothpick inserted in the center comes out clean.

Cool in pan for 10 minutes. Invert onto serving plate and allow to cool completely. Dust with icing sugar, if desired.

Cherry Pie Filling

Use this as a filling for a full-sized pie or little tarts, fold it into phyllo triangles (see p. 251), dollop over Vanilla Ice Cream (p. 206), spread it over a cheesecake, or just eat it off a spoon (I won't tell!) This irresistible filling is enhanced with a subtle hit of cinnamon. It's just the thing to make when your cherry tree—or farmer's market— is loaded with fresh fruit.

MAKES 2 CUPS (500 ML)
Preparation time: *20 minutes +*
15 minutes cooling time
Cooking time: *15 minutes*

3 cups (750 mL) stoned and halved sweet cherries
¼ cup (60 mL) + 2 tbsp sugar
1½ tsp vanilla extract
1½ tsp lemon juice
1 3-in (8-cm) cinnamon stick
2 tbsp arrowroot powder (see p. 250)

In a medium saucepan on medium-high heat, combine cherries, ¼ cup (60 mL) water, sugar, vanilla, lemon juice, and cinnamon stick. Stir constantly until sugar has dissolved, then allow to boil, stirring occasionally, for 15 minutes to cook fruit and thicken sauce. Remove cinnamon stick. Remove saucepan from heat.

In a small bowl, combine arrowroot powder with 2 tbsp water, then stir into fruit until completely dissolved.

Let sit at room temperature for about 15 minutes to thicken. Mash with a fork to break up some cherries before using.

Berry Swirl Cheesecake

Creamy, luscious, and oozing berry goodness, this cake, with a refined sugar-free filling, is just sweet enough to end your meal without making you feel overly full. The crust is quite firm and chewy, which contrasts well with the creamy topping. Best if you make this a day in advance to allow time for overnight chilling.

MAKES 10–12 SERVINGS

Preparation time: *30 minutes + 1 hour chilling*

Cooking time: *75 minutes + cooling time + 8 hours/overnight chilling*

CRUST

2 cups (500 mL or 1 pt) vegan graham cracker, or other cookie, crumbs

½ cup (125 mL) all-purpose flour

½ cup (C125 mL) canola oil

¼ cup (60 mL) brown rice syrup (see p. 250)

1 tsp vanilla extract

BERRY SAUCE

3 cups (750 mL) fresh or frozen berries (if using strawberries, hull and halve)

¼ cup (60 mL) brown rice syrup

2 tsp arrowroot powder (see p. 250)

FILLING

8 oz (230 g) vegan cream cheese

6 oz (175 g) soft regular tofu (water-packed)

8 oz (230 g) firm regular tofu (water-packed)

¾ cup (185 mL) brown rice syrup

2 tbsp arrowroot powder

1½ tsp vanilla extract

¼ tsp salt

Make crust

Lightly spray an 8-in (20-cm) spring-form pan with non-stick spray.

In a large bowl, mix together cookie crumbs and flour. Make a well in center and add oil, syrup, and vanilla. Mix to combine well.

Press mixture firmly into pan and chill for at least 1 hour.

Make sauce

In a medium saucepan, combine berries, syrup, and arrowroot powder. On medium heat, bring to a boil, stirring constantly until all liquid is released. Reduce heat to medium and cook for 10 minutes, until thickened and soft.

Remove from heat, and cool for 15 minutes, to room temperature. Strain through a sieve, if desired, for a smoother, seed-free sauce. Set aside ½ cup (125 mL) sauce.

Make filling

Preheat oven to 350°F (180°C).

In a blender or food processor, blend cream cheese and tofus for 5–8 minutes, until very smooth and creamy. Scrape down sides of blender as required. Add syrup, arrowroot powder, vanilla, and salt and continue to process until very well mixed. Pour over crust and spread evenly to edges.

With a 1-tbsp measure, dot reserved ½ cup (125 mL) berry sauce over cheesecake. With a knife, skewer, or chopstick, swirl sauce into filling, creating a pretty pattern.

Bake for about 75 minutes, until edges are lightly browned and have pulled away from edges of pan. Edges will be firmer than center, which will be a little wobbly when pan is shaken.

Turn off oven, crack open door and let sit for 30 minutes in cooling oven before removing. Cool in pan at room temperature. Store overnight in refrigerator to completely set before serving.

Serve with remaining berry sauce.

Variation: Use 1 cup (250 mL) Cherry Pie Filling (p. 215) blended until smooth in place of Berry Sauce.

Maple & Walnut Cheesecake

I serve this rich and creamy cheesecake made with maple syrup, the unofficial flavor of Canada, at our annual Canada Day family barbecue. Make it a day in advance to allow for overnight chilling.

MAKES 1 8-IN (20-CM) CHEESECAKE, OR 10–12 SERVINGS

Preparation time: *15 minutes + 1 hour chilling*

Cooking time: *45 minutes + 8 hours/ overnight cooling*

CRUST

1⅓ cups (330 mL) vegan graham cracker or other plain cookie crumbs

½ cup (125 mL) minced walnuts

⅓ cup (80 mL) canola oil

2 tbsp maple syrup

1 tsp vanilla extract

½ tsp maple extract

FILLING

8 oz (230 g) vegan cream cheese

6 oz (175 g) soft regular tofu (water-packed)

8 oz (230 g) firm regular tofu (water-packed)

½ cup (125 mL) maple syrup

½ cup (125 mL) light brown sugar

¼ cup (60 mL) cornstarch

1 tsp white balsamic vinegar (see p. 252)

1 tsp maple extract

½ tsp vanilla extract

1 cup (250 mL) walnut pieces

Make crust

Lightly spray an 8-in (20-cm) springform pan with non-stick cooking spray.

In a large bowl, combine cookie crumbs and walnuts.

In a medium bowl, whisk together oil, syrup, and extracts. Stir into crumb mixture and mix to combine well. Press firmly into prepared pan.

Place in refrigerator to chill for 1 hour before using.

Make filling

Preheat oven to 350°F (180°C).

In a blender or food processor, purée cream cheese and both measures of tofu until very smooth and creamy. Stop to scrape down sides of blender as required.

Add maple syrup, sugar, cornstarch, vinegar, maple extract, and vanilla extract. Continue blending until completely mixed. Add walnuts and pulse a few times.

Pour filling over crust and smooth top.

Bake for 45 minutes, until edges are lightly browned and have pulled away from edges of pan. Edges will be firmer than center, which will be a little wobbly when pan is shaken.

Turn off oven, crack open door, and let sit for 30 minutes in cooling oven before removing.

Remove from oven and cool in pan, on a rack, for at least 1 hour until completely cool. Store overnight in refrigerator to completely set before serving.

Chilled Blueberry Chocolate Pie

This is the pie my husband regularly requests for Father's Day. The combination of blueberries and chocolate ganache is refreshing and yet rich. Make a day in advance to allow for overnight chilling.

MAKES 1 9-IN (23-CM) PIE OR 10–12 SERVINGS

Preparation time: 45 minutes + 3–8 hours chilling

g *(pie crust only)*

s

⅓ cup (80 mL) plain soy milk

1 tbsp maple syrup

¾ cup (185 mL) vegan semi-sweet chocolate chips

1 pre-baked 9-in (23-cm) pie crust

3 cups (750 mL) frozen blueberries

2 tbsp sugar

2 tbsp maple syrup

1 tsp agar powder (see p. 250)

1 cup (250 mL) frozen blueberries

In a small saucepan on medium-high heat, combine soy milk, 1 tbsp syrup, and chocolate chips, stirring until dissolved. Pour mix into pre-baked pie crust and chill in refrigerator for at least 1 hour.

In a large saucepan on medium-high heat, combine blueberries, sugar, 2 tbsp syrup, and 1 cup (250 mL) water and bring to a boil. Reduce heat to medium and simmer, stirring occasionally, for 25–30 minutes until reduced and thick.

Combine agar with 2 tbsp water, then add to berry mix. Stir for 2 minutes to combine well.

Stir in final cup of blueberries and mix well. Pour over chocolate layer. Chill in refrigerator for at least 3 hours or overnight.

COOKIES ARE A PERFECTLY PItemTABLE *treat for summer indulging, quick and (usually) easy to make, so a sweet snack or dessert is never far away. A refreshing, if untraditional, way to enjoy cookies in the summer (other than as ice cream sandwiches) is to make frozen cookie dough balls. Just roll the prepared dough into 1-tbsp sized balls and freeze on a baking sheet, then when you feel like a cold, sweet pick-me-up, pop one straight from the freezer into your mouth. Fun for a summertime kid's party!*

cookies

Chocolate Peanut Chunk Cookies

Are my children the only allergy-free kids in the world who don't like peanut butter? If you also have peanut-haters in the house, just replace the nuts in this recipe with chocolate chunks—the peanut butter taste is pretty subtle. These cookies are thin and chewy, softer if baked for 10 minutes, and crispier if baked for 12, and really good, no matter how you feel about peanuts.

MAKES ABOUT 18 COOKIES
Preparation time: 10 minutes
Cooking time: 10–12 minutes

1 cup (250 mL) sugar

3 tbsp vegan margarine

3 tbsp natural, smooth peanut butter

¼ cup (60 mL) plain soy milk

1 tsp chocolate or vanilla extract

1 cup (250 mL) all-purpose flour

3 tbsp Dutch processed cocoa powder

1 tbsp ground flaxseeds

¼ tsp baking powder

¼ tsp baking soda

¼ tsp salt

⅓ cup (80 mL) vegan chocolate chunks or chips

⅓ cup (80 mL) roasted salted peanuts

Preheat oven to 375°F (190°C). Line 2 large baking sheets with parchment paper.

In a large bowl, cream sugar, margarine, and peanut butter for 3–4 minutes until combined well. *Note*: Mixture won't become light and fluffy like a creaming mix.

Add soy milk and extract and mix to combine. Sift in flour, cocoa powder, flaxseeds, baking powder, baking soda, and salt and mix to combine. Fold in chocolate chunks and peanuts.

Drop dough by the tbsp 2 in (5 cm) apart onto sheets. Flatten a little with bottom of a measuring cup slightly dampened or sprayed with non-stick spray.

Bake for 10–12 minutes until puffy and lightly browned around edges. Cool on sheets for 5 minutes, then transfer to a rack to complete cooling.

Spicy Spelt Chocolate Chip Cookies

My children asked me to make chocolate chip cookies one day, but I didn't have any all-purpose flour in the house, so I created these. I think spelt pairs well with the warm spiciness of ancho chili powder, which adds a hint of heat to these big, soft, chewy, yet not too sweet cookies. For more kick, add additional chili flakes.

MAKES ABOUT 18 COOKIES
Preparation time: 40 minutes
Baking time: 10–12 minutes

½ cup (125 mL) almond milk

½ cup (125 mL) sugar

¼ cup (60 mL) packed light brown sugar

¼ cup (60 mL) maple syrup

2 tbsp canola oil

2 tbsp ground flaxseeds

½ tsp vanilla extract

½ tsp caramel or vanilla extract

2½ cups (625 mL) spelt flour (see p. 250)

1½ tsp ancho chili powder (see p. 250)

½ tsp baking soda

½ tsp salt

½ tsp ground cinnamon

¼ tsp chili flakes (optional)

1 cup (250 mL) vegan chocolate chips

In a large mixing bowl, whisk together milk, sugars, syrup, oil, flaxseeds, and extracts for 2 minutes, until smooth. Let sit for 5 minutes. Sift in flour, chili powder, baking soda, salt, cinnamon, and chili flakes and mix until just combined. Fold in chocolate chips. Cover and refrigerate for 30 minutes.

Preheat oven to 350°F (180°C). Line 2 large baking sheets with parchment paper.

With slightly dampened hands, roll dough into 2-in (5-cm) sized balls. Flatten between palms, and place 2 in (5 cm) apart on baking sheets. Bake for 10–12 minutes until cookies are puffy and bottoms slightly browned.

Cool for 5 minutes on sheets, then transfer to a rack to complete cooling.

Masa Chocolate Chip Cookies

Not just for tamales anymore, masa harina adds brilliant texture and flavor to these soft cookies. The paprika and cinnamon combine to make a spice profile that will have your friends wondering just what you put in these to make them so good!

MAKES ABOUT 14 COOKIES
Preparation time: 10 minutes
Cooking time: 10–12 minutes

⅔ cup (160 mL) sugar

¼ cup (60 mL) canola oil

2 tbsp vegan shortening

2 tbsp agave (see p. 250)

2 tbsp almond milk

1 tsp vanilla extract

¾ cup (185 mL) all-purpose flour

½ cup (125 mL) masa harina (see p. 251)

½ tsp baking powder

½ tsp ground cinnamon

½ tsp salt

¼ tsp smoked paprika

½ cup (125 mL) vegan chocolate chips

Preheat oven to 350°F (180°C). Line 2 large baking sheets with parchment paper.

In a large bowl, cream together sugar, oil, shortening, and agave for 3–4 minutes, until thick and shiny. Beat in milk and extract.

Sift in flour, masa harina, baking powder, cinnamon, salt, and paprika. Mix to form a soft dough. Stir in chocolate chips.

Scoop heaped 1-tbsp measures of dough and roll into balls. Flatten between palms to form 2-in (5-cm) cookies, then place 2 in (5 cm) apart on prepared sheets. Bake for 10–12 minutes, until bottoms are browned but cookies still soft.

Cool on sheets for 5 minutes, then transfer to a rack to complete cooling.

Cherry & Almond Cookies (opposite)

Chai Tea Cookies (p. 230)

Basil & Blueberry Cookies (p. 228)

Lavender Cookies (p. 229)

Cherry & Almond Cookies

Cherries and almonds are best friends—cookie BFFs, in fact. Once you try these, you'll agree.

MAKES ABOUT 22 COOKIES
Preparation time: 1 hour, 40 minutes, including making paste and chilling
Cooking time: 10–12 minutes

½ cup (125 mL) dried cherries

½ cup (125 mL) sugar

¼ cup (60 mL) canola oil

2 tbsp almond milk

½ tsp vanilla extract

½ tsp almond extract

1¼ cups (310 mL) all-purpose flour

¼ cup (60 mL) ground almonds

½ tsp salt

½ tsp baking soda

½ tsp ground cinnamon

½ cup (125 mL) slivered almonds, to garnish

In a medium saucepan, soak dried cherries in ¾ cup (185 mL) water for at least 1 hour. On high heat, bring to a boil. Reduce heat to medium and cook, uncovered, and at a boil for 10 minutes. Add water 1 tbsp at a time, if required to stop mixture from sticking. Remove from heat and mash to form an uneven, thick paste. Let sit for about 10 minutes, until cooled to room temperature.

Stir in sugar, oil, milk, and extracts and mix to combine well. Sift in flour, ground almonds, salt, baking soda, and cinnamon and mix to just combine. Cover pan and chill in refrigerator for at least 15 minutes.

Preheat oven to 375°F (190°C). Line 2 large baking sheets with parchment paper.

Scoop heaped 1-tbsp measures of dough and roll into balls. Flatten to form 2-in (5-cm) cookies and place 2 in (5 cm) apart on prepared sheets. Press 1 tsp slivered almonds into top of each cookie. Bake for 10–12 minutes until puffy and just browned at edges.

Cool on sheets for 5 minutes, then transfer to a rack to complete cooling.

Basil & Blueberry Cookies

I made these for my elder daughter to take to school and share with her class on her birthday, but asked the teacher to keep the basil a secret. She told the children that these were "blueberry cookies," and they gobbled up the lot. (The basil flavor is more apparent if you know it's there.)

MAKES ABOUT 15 COOKIES
Preparation time: *30 minutes, including chilling time*
Cooking time: *12–14 minutes*

¼ cup (60 mL) plain soy milk

¼ cup (60 mL) packed fresh basil leaves

¾ cup (185 mL) sugar

¼ cup (60 mL) canola oil

½ tsp vanilla extract

¼ tsp strawberry or vanilla extract

1¼ cups (310 mL) all-purpose flour

½ tsp salt

½ tsp baking soda

2 tbsp dried blueberries

2 tbsp fresh or frozen and thawed blueberries

In a medium saucepan on medium heat, scald milk. Remove from heat. Roughly crush fresh basil between your fingers and add to milk. Cover and let steep for 15 minutes as it cools to room temperature.

Remove basil leaves and squeeze them over saucepan to extract any remaining flavored milk. Whisk in sugar, oil, and extracts, until thick. Sift in flour, salt, and baking soda and mix to form a firm dough. Stir in dried and fresh blueberries. Chill in refrigerator for 20 minutes.

Preheat oven to 375°F (190°C). Line 2 large baking sheets with parchment paper.

Scoop heaped 1-tbsp measures of dough and roll into balls. Flatten to form 2-in (5-cm) cookies and place 2 in (5 cm) apart on prepared sheets. Bake for 12–14 minutes, until puffy with lightly browned edges.

Cool on sheets for 5 minutes, then transfer to a rack to complete cooling.

Lavender Cookies

My daughter—who is not keen on anything "weird"—ate two of these cookies and said, "I can't believe I'm eating flowers!" And she'd have eaten more if I hadn't stopped her. These gently flavored cookies are light, soft, and almost like shortbread (it's the rice flour), and are perfect for an elegant garden party.

MAKES ABOUT 18 COOKIES
Preparation time: 20 minutes
Cooking time: 10–12 minutes

¼ cup (60 mL) plain soy milk

¼ cup (60 mL) fresh culinary-grade lavender flowers

¾ cup (185 mL) sugar

2 tbsp vegan shortening

2 tbsp coconut oil, room temperature

¼ tsp vanilla extract

1 cup (250 mL) all-purpose flour

½ cup (125 mL) white rice flour (see p. 251)

½ tsp salt

½ tsp baking soda

1 tbsp finely chopped, fresh lavender flowers (optional)

Preheat oven to 350°F (180°C). Line 2 large baking sheets with parchment paper.

In a small saucepan on medium-high heat, scald milk. Remove from heat and stir in lavender. Cover and let steep for 15 minutes, while milk cools to room temperature.

In a large bowl, cream together sugar, shortening, oil, and vanilla for 3–4 minutes, until light and fluffy. Strain milk through medium sieve over bowl. Press lavender to extract all the flavored milk. Mix to combine well. Sift in flours, salt, and baking soda and mix until dough forms. Stir in 1 tbsp lavender flowers.

Scoop heaped 1-tbsp measures of dough and roll into balls. Flatten to form 2-in (5-cm) cookies and place 2 in (5 cm) apart on prepared sheets. Bake for 10–12 minutes, until slightly puffy, with pale bottoms.

Cool on sheets for 5 minutes, then transfer to a rack to complete cooling.

Culinary-grade lavender hasn't been treated in any way, sprayed with chemicals, or preserved.

Chai Tea Cookies

Serve with a cup of tea, hot or iced, chai or other, for a mid-afternoon treat. These tea- and spice-enhanced cookies also make great ice cream sandwiches when filled with Vanilla Ice Cream (p. 206)!

MAKES ABOUT 28 COOKIES

Preparation time: 30 minutes, including chilling

Cooking time: 10–12 minutes

⅓ cup (80 mL) almond milk

2 chai tea bags

½ cup (125 mL) light brown sugar, packed

¼ cup (60 mL) canola oil

¼ cup (60 mL) brown rice syrup (see p. 250)

½ tsp vanilla extract

1¾ cups (415 mL) all-purpose flour

2 tbsp cornstarch

½ tsp salt

½ tsp baking powder

1 chai tea bag, contents only, 1 tsp

In a medium saucepan on medium heat, scald milk. Remove from heat. Add tea bags, cover, and let steep for 15 minutes while milk cools to room temperature.

Remove teabags and squeeze to extract any remaining flavored milk. Whisk in sugar, oil, syrup, and vanilla for 2–3 minutes, until smooth. Sift in flour, cornstarch, salt, baking powder, and tea bag contents and mix until a firm dough forms. Place pan in refrigerator to chill for at least 20 minutes.

Preheat oven to 375°F (190°C). Line large baking sheets with parchment paper.

Turn dough onto lightly floured surface. With a lightly floured rolling pin, roll out to ¼-in (6-mm) thick. With a 2-in (5-cm) or shaped cookie cutter, cut out cookies, and place 2-in (5-cm) apart on prepared sheets. Re-roll dough scraps and cut out additional cookies. Bake for 10–12 minutes until puffy, firm to the touch, with lightly browned bottoms.

Cool on sheets for 5 minutes, then transfer to a rack to cool.

Espresso Cookies

With a hit of caffeine, these cookies are just right for a mid-afternoon pick-me-up. The cookie dough isn't overly sweet, so the sugar sprinkles pleasantly balance the flavor of coffee.

MAKES ABOUT 18 COOKIES

Preparation time: 10 minutes
Cooking time: 10–12 minutes

  (in margarine)

¾ cup (185 mL) packed light brown sugar

¼ cup (60 mL) vegan shortening

¼ cup (60 mL) vegan margarine

¼ cup (60 mL) very strong espresso, room temperature (or 3 tbsp instant coffee dissolved in ¼ cup [60 mL] boiling water), decaf if desired

½ tsp vanilla extract

1½ cups (375 mL) all-purpose flour

¼ cup (60 mL) whole wheat pastry or all-purpose flour

2 tbsp cornstarch

2 tsp instant coffee, or espresso powder, decaf if desired

½ tsp baking powder

½ tsp salt

¼ tsp baking soda

½ cup (125 mL) turbinado sugar (see note, right)

Preheat oven to 375°F (190°C). Line 2 large baking sheets with parchment paper.

In a large bowl, cream sugar, shortening, and margarine for 3–4 minutes, until thick and creamy. Beat in espresso and extract. (Mixture will look curdled at this point.) Sift in flours, cornstarch, instant coffee, baking powder, salt, and baking soda and mix to form a soft dough.

Scoop heaped 1-tbsp measures of dough and roll into balls. Flatten to form 2-in (5-cm) cookies and place 2 in (5 cm) apart on prepared sheets. Sprinkle turbinado sugar over each cookie. Bake for 10–12 minutes, until bottoms are browned but cookies are still soft.

Cool on sheets for 5 minutes, then transfer to a rack to complete cooling.

Turbinado sugar is made from pure cane sugar extract; it's also known as "sugar in the raw."

Banana Cookies

Before I wrote my own cookbooks, I was a recipe tester for other authors. While testing for Terry Hope Romero (co-author of Veganomicon), I learned this method of reducing a fruit or vegetable purée. I wondered if the method would work for bananas—here's tasty proof that it does.

MAKES ABOUT 18 COOKIES

Preparation time: 40 minutes including reducing banana

Cooking time: 10–12 minutes

 **S** (margarine only)

g

2 very ripe medium bananas
¼ cup (60 mL) maple syrup
¼ cup (60 mL) vegan margarine
¼ cup (60 mL) vegan shortening
½ cup (125 mL) packed light brown sugar
¼ tsp vanilla extract
1 cup (250 mL) + 1 tbsp all-purpose flour
½ tsp baking soda
½ tsp salt

In a small saucepan, mash bananas and syrup together with a fork until very few small lumps remain.

On medium heat, bring to a simmer uncovered for 20 minutes until darkened, thick, and jam-like. Stir frequently to prevent sticking, especially at end of cooking time. Purée will reduce to about ⅓ cup (80 mL). Refrigerate in saucepan for 10 minutes, or cool on countertop for at least 30 minutes, until room temperature.

Preheat oven to 350°F (180°C). Line 2 large baking sheets with parchment paper.

In a large bowl, cream together margarine, shortening, and sugar for 3–4 minutes, until light and creamy. Stir in vanilla and banana mixture. Sift in flour, baking soda, and salt and mix to form a soft dough.

Scoop heaped 1-tbsp measure of dough and roll into balls. Flatten to 2-in (5-cm) cookies, and place 2 in (5 cm) apart on prepared sheets. Bake for 10–12 minutes until puffy, with browned edges and soft middle. Cookies will firm as they cool.

Cool on sheets for 5 minutes, then transfer to a rack to complete cooling.

Sugar-free Sugar Cookies

It looks like a sugar cookie and tastes like a sugar cookie, so it must be a sugar cookie, right? Nope, there isn't any granulated sugar in these mouth-watering treats.

MAKES ABOUT 18 COOKIES
Preparation time: 10 minutes
Cooking time: 8–10 minutes

2 tbsp vegan margarine

2 tbsp vegan shortening

2 tbsp coconut oil, room temperature

¼ cup (60 mL) brown rice syrup (see p. 250)

¼ cup (60 mL) agave (see p. 250)

1 tsp vanilla extract

2 tbsp vanilla or plain soy milk

1¼ cups (310 mL) all-purpose flour

⅓ cup (80 mL) white rice flour (see p. 251)

½ tsp baking powder

½ tsp salt

Preheat oven to 350°F (180°C). Line 2 large baking sheets with parchment paper.

In a large bowl, whisk together margarine, shortening, and oil for 2–3 minutes, until smooth and creamy. Whisk in syrup and agave until thick. Whisk in vanilla and soy milk.

Sift in flour, baking powder, and salt, and mix gently until just combined to form a soft, sticky dough.

(*Tip*: Spray a 1-tbsp measure with non-stick spray.)

Drop dough by the tbsp, 2 in (5 cm) apart, onto prepared sheets. Flatten gently with bottom of a measuring cup dampened with water or sprayed with non-stick spray. Bake for 8–10 minutes, until bottoms are just golden.

Cool on sheets for 5 minutes, then transfer to a rack to complete cooling.

Nut & Seed Gluten-free Cookies

I often send cookies to my daughter's dance class for a shared treat. One day she asked me to make special cookies for a classmate who couldn't "eat flour" and "always misses out on the treats." I checked with the girl's mother, and "can't eat flour" is kid-speak for gluten-free. From then on, I have always sent a gluten-free option, including these made with white rice and millet flours, to class. The cookies are a little delicate straight out of the oven.

MAKES ABOUT 18 COOKIES
Preparation time: 45 minutes including chilling
Cooking time: 10–12 minutes

2 tbsp raw pumpkin seeds

2 tbsp raw sunflower seeds

2 tbsp hemp seeds (see p. 251)

¾ cup (185 mL) packed light brown sugar

¼ cup (60 mL) almond milk

1 tbsp ground flaxseeds

1 tsp ground chia seeds (see p. 250)

2 tbsp tahini (see p. 252)

½ tsp vanilla extract

¼ tsp almond extract

¼ cup (60 mL) + 2 tbsp white rice flour (see p. 251)

¼ cup (60 mL) + 2 tbsp millet flour (see p. 251)

¼ cup (60 mL) ground pecans

¼ cup (60 mL) ground almonds

2 tbsp cornstarch

1 tsp baking powder

½ tsp salt

½ cup (125 mL) roughly chopped almonds or pecans

Preheat oven to 350°F (180°C). Line 2 large baking sheets with parchment paper and spray with non-stick spray (as cookies are sticky).

In a spice grinder or powerful blender, pulse together pumpkin, sunflower, and hemp seeds for 2–3 minutes, until a fine, flour-like powder forms. Do not over-process into butter. Set aside.

In a large bowl, whisk together sugar, almond milk, flaxseeds, and chia seeds for 2–3 minutes, until combined well. Let sit for 10 minutes, then whisk again until shiny. Beat in tahini and extracts.

Sift in ground seed mixture, flours, ground pecans and almonds, cornstarch, baking powder, and salt, and mix to form a thick, sticky dough. Stir in chopped nuts. Cover dough and chill in refrigerator for at least 30 minutes.

Scoop heaped 1-tbsp measures of dough and roll into balls. Flatten to form 2-in (5-cm) cookies and place 2 in (5 cm) apart on prepared sheets. Bake for 10–12 minutes, until puffy and slightly cracked with lightly golden edges.

Cool on sheets for 5 minutes, then carefully transfer to a rack to complete cooling.

No Bake Oatmeal Cookies

These are a little fragile, but the magic that is coconut oil helps them to firm up in the refrigerator. If you don't flatten them into cookie shapes but leave them as balls, just call them truffles.

MAKES 16–18 COOKIES
Preparation time: *15 minutes*
Cooling time: *15 minutes*

n *(optional)*

g

s

¼ cup (60 mL) vegan margarine

3 tbsp canola oil

3 tbsp coconut oil, room temperature

1 cup (250 mL) + 2 tbsp vegan graham cracker crumbs

¾ cup (185 mL) quick-cooking rolled oats

½ cup (125 mL) icing (confectioner's) sugar

¼ cup (60 mL) raisins, chopped nuts, chocolate chips, or a mixture

1 tbsp plain soy milk (optional)

1 cup (250 mL) melted vegan chocolate

Line a large plate or small baking sheet with parchment paper.

In a small saucepan on medium heat, combine margarine and oils and cook for 5 minutes, stirring constantly, until margarine has melted.

In a large bowl, combine crumbs, oats, sugar, and raisins, nuts, or chocolate chips. Pour melted mixture into dry ingredients and mix to combine well. With dampened hands, squeeze to form generous 1-tbsp sized balls. If mixture doesn't easily form into balls, mix in soy milk, 1 tsp at a time. Flatten to form 2-in (5-cm) cookies and place on sheet. Place in freezer for 15 minutes to set.

Dip half of each cookie into melted chocolate or drizzle over each cookie. Place on plate or sheet, then refrigerate for 20–30 minutes to set.

Once chocolate is set, store cookies in a covered container in refrigerator.

No Bake Oatmeal Bars

Press mixture into an 8 x 8-in (2-L square) pan and chill in the freezer for 15 minutes before cutting into 16 equal pieces. Drizzle with melted chocolate and store in a covered container in refrigerator.

IN THIS CHAPTER, YOU'LL

FIND *a selection of thirst-quenching options to refresh your body while enlivening your taste buds. Serve them over ice, chilled, or at room temperature. I'm not much of a drinker, but an ice-cold (vegan) beer is among the very best beverages for a summer picnic or barbecue—the key words are ice and cold! A chilled glass of white wine (straight up or as a spritzer) is also light and refreshing. The wonderful online resource Barnivore.com offers the best vegan options for alcoholic drinks in your area. There's even an app for your phone. Of course, the most important thing to drink, especially in summer when your body loses moisture through perspiration, is lots of fresh, clean water!*

drinks

Water that wows!

Add any of the following to a pitcher of (clean and filtered) still or sparkling water and keep in the refrigerator or by the picnic table for a refreshing and flavorful al fresco beverage:

- ice cubes made from pure fruit juice
- ice cubes made from water infused with fresh herbs; mint and basil are especially refreshing
- frozen grapes or berries, frozen chopped mangos, or other frozen fruit pieces
- sprigs of fresh herbs such as mint, thyme, or basil
- citrus fruit slices: lemon, lime, orange, grapefruit
- crushed lemongrass stalks
- fresh ginger slices
- cucumber slices
- kiwifruit slices

Ginger Lemonade

Made without refined sugar, this is a slightly tart and very refreshing twist on lemonade.

MAKES ABOUT 12 CUPS (3 L)
Preparation time: *30 minutes + chilling time.*

1½ cups (375 mL) fresh lemon juice

3 tbsp lemon zest

1 cup (250 mL) brown rice syrup (see p. 250)

½ cup (125 mL) agave (see p. 250)

1 lemongrass stalk, crushed (optional)

1 2-in (5-cm) piece fresh ginger, peeled and scored

8–10 cups (2–2.5 L) water, plain or sparkling, or sparkling white wine, to taste

In a medium saucepan, combine lemon juice and zest, brown rice syrup, agave, lemongrass, and ginger with 1½ cups (375 mL) water on medium-high heat and bring to a brisk simmer. Reduce heat to medium-low and cook, stirring occasionally, for 15–20 minutes (or longer, if required), until flavors meld and mixture is slightly syrupy. Remove from heat and cool to room temperature.

Strain out zest, lemongrass, and ginger. Pour liquid into jar or pitcher and chill in refrigerator. Before serving, stir into cold water, sparkling water, or wine; I use about ½ cup (125 mL) syrup to 2 cups (500 mL) water.

Lemon Barley Water

This is an English summer treat, which I remember my gran making for us when we were little. It is very refreshing, especially if made with sparkling water.

MAKES 4 CUPS (1 L)
Preparation time: *10 minutes + overnight (8 hours) soaking*

g

½ cup (125 mL) pearl barley
1 medium lemon, sliced
¼ cup (60 mL) agave (see p. 250)
additional lemon slices, to garnish

In a large bowl or pitcher, soak barley and lemon slices overnight in 4 cups (1 L) water, still or sparkling. Strain out barley (use it in a recipe such as Hearty Three-Grain Salad, p. 147) and reserve water.

Remove lemon slices and squeeze to extract flavored water. Discard soaked slices. Stir in agave until combined well.

Add more clean water, as desired, to dilute to taste. Chill in refrigerator. Serve with fresh slices of lemon.

Variation: Use different citrus fruits, such as orange, lime, or grapefruit, to flavor the barley water.

Rhubarb Water

Another traditional English recipe (my cultural roots are showing!). This is a balance of sweet and mouth-puckering and, as such, is very refreshing.

MAKES 3 CUPS (750 mL)
Preparation time: 25 minutes + 1 hour, 30 minutes chilling

2 cups (500 mL) chopped rhubarb
¾ cup (185 mL) sugar

In a large saucepan on medium heat, combine rhubarb, sugar, and 3 cups (750 mL) water, still or sparkling, and simmer for about 15 minutes, until rhubarb is broken up and tender.

Strain out rhubarb and reserve water (dollop cooked rhubarb over Vanilla Ice Cream, p. 206).

Cool for 30 minutes to room temperature, then chill in refrigerator for at least 1 hour. Add more water to dilute, to taste.

Variation: Use another summer fruit, such as pears or peaches.

Limoncello Lemonade

My recipe tester Debyi Kucera says that this drink is so refreshing, you almost forget there is alcohol in it—so watch out! Serve in a champagne glass rimmed with sugar or on the rocks in a high-ball glass, also rimmed with sugar. (Thanks, Debyi, for sharing this recipe!)

(Note: If you want to use homemade limoncello, make it at least 1 week in advance.)

MAKES 1 SERVING

Preparation time: 20 minutes + cooling, not including time to make limoncello

3 tbsp agave (see p. 250)

4 tsp lemon juice

2 tbsp citrus vodka

2 tbsp limoncello liqueur, store-bought or home-made (right)

½ cup (125 mL) Ginger Lemonade (p. 241)

2 cups (500 mL) ice

....

In a small saucepan on medium-high heat, bring ¼ cup (60 mL) hot water, agave, and lemon juice to a boil. Boil for 5 minutes, stirring occasionally, to make lemon simple-syrup. Remove from heat and let cool for 30 minutes.

In a blender on high speed, combine syrup, vodka, limoncello, lemonade, and ice until ice is crushed.

Limoncello

MAKES 5 CUPS (1.25 L)

5 large or 10 small lemons, preferably organic

4¼ cups (1.06 L) vodka

2½ cups (625 mL) sugar

Wash lemons in cool water to remove dirt. With a vegetable peeler or sharp knife, peel lemons, leaving as little white pith on zest as possible.

In a large resealable jar or container, combine peels and vodka. Set in a cool place for 7 days, giving it a little swirl once a day. The alcohol will become darker each day. After 7 days, strain vodka through a coffee filter or cheesecloth. Discard peel.

In a large saucepan, bring 5½ cups (1.85 L) water and sugar to a boil. Boil for 5 minutes, stirring occasionally. Let cool for 15 minutes. Mix sugar syrup with vodka.

Pour into bottles or containers and cool completely. Stored in freezer until ready to serve, this should keep for up to 1 year.

Variation: Use lime instead of lemon juice and make limoncello (as above) with lime peel.

Iced Tea

The classic accompaniment to any al fresco meal, iced tea is very easy to make at home, and it's not as cloyingly sweet as most commercial iced tea mixes. You can make it the night before, so the tea is well-steeped, or make it the morning of your picnic.

MAKES ABOUT 8 SERVINGS

3 tea bags (black tea, green tea, mint tea, fruit infusion, etc.)
⅓ cup (80 mL) sugar

In a large pitcher, combine teabags, 6 cups (1.5 L) boiling water and sugar, and stir to dissolve sugar. Cool for 30 minutes, to room temperature.

At this point, either refrigerate overnight or finish preparing tea: Remove tea bags from pitcher and squeeze over pitcher to remove any remaining liquid. Dilute with additional water, to taste, and add flavoring (see below), as desired.

Add other flavors after the tea has cooled to room temperature:

- sprigs of fresh herbs such as mint, thyme, or basil
- sliced citrus fruits (lemon, lime, orange, grapefruit)
- berries
- sliced peaches or apples or other fruit
- crushed lemongrass stalks
- lemon juice
- vegan milk
- slices of fresh ginger

Iced Coffee

This is so easy! Make extra coffee in the morning so that you have enough to take with you on your picnic or to serve to your backyard brunch guests. Adjust the strength to taste—you can even make it decaf. To serve, add ice cubes, additional sweetener, and vegan milk, as desired.

MAKES 6 CUPS (1.5 L)

6 cups (1.5 L) freshly brewed coffee

⅓ cup (80 mL) sugar

In a large pitcher, combine coffee and sugar and stir to dissolve sugar. Cool for 30 minutes to room temperature.

Blend iced coffee with Vanilla (p. 206) or Triple Chocolate (p. 209) Ice Cream for a frothy coffee shake.

Smoothies

Cold smoothies are great at picnics or as a refreshing after-hike treat. Since almost any fruit can be used in a smoothie, creativity is the name of the game. Here are a few pointers.

- I'm firmly in the "no ice" camp; ice only dilutes the flavors. Instead, I like to cool my smoothie by adding peeled and frozen ripe bananas (or other ripe fruits such as berries) that I've stored in single-serve ziplock bags in the freezer.
- A powerful blender is your best friend for making smoothies, but any blender will work; you may need to give the motor a few breaks as you blend.
- I often add applesauce, water, or soy or another non-dairy milk to my smoothies. For a more dessert-like version, I add the odd scoop of non-dairy ice cream.
- Most fruit smoothies don't need it, but if you want to sweeten to taste, use a natural and neutral-tasting liquid sweetener such as agave or brown rice syrup.
- Add a scoop of vegan protein powder, wheat germ, flax-, hemp-, or chia-seeds or their oils, or nut butters to smoothies for a boost of protein or omega-3 healthy fatty acids.
- Make smoothies just before you're ready to head off to the picnic; pack in a well-sealed container to prevent leakage, and in ice, to keep them cool.

Here are a few smoothie flavor combinations to try:

- strawberry, bananas, and peaches
- apples, kale, bananas, soy milk, frozen peaches, and mangos
- soy milk, smooth peanut butter, chocolate syrup or melted chocolate chips, and frozen bananas
- strawberries, bananas, pineapple, and a little chocolate sauce
- peaches, orange juice, and vanilla extract
- orange juice, soy milk, vanilla yogurt, frozen mangos or peaches, with optional Vanilla Ice Cream (p. 206)
- cherries, kale, and cocoa powder
- cherries, strawberries, blueberries, and spinach
- peaches with vanilla-flavored soy milk or vanilla extract

appendices

SPECIAL ·
INGREDIENTS

THEME MENUS ·
FOR PICNICS
& BARBECUES

ALLERGEN ·
LIST

Special Ingredients

Wherever possible in Vegan al Fresco, *I use supermarket-friendly, easy-to-find ingredients (bearing in mind that what might be easy for me might not be for you). Here is a list of "not commonplace but still available in my neighborhood" ingredients used in the book.*

Agar
Also known as agar-agar, it's a gelatinous material made from a sea vegetable. It's available to purchase in sticks, as flakes, or as a powder; I use the powdered form. If you can find only the sticks or flakes, pulse in a spice grinder or blender to form a powder.

Agave
A natural sweetener made from the sap of the agave (the plant from which tequila is distilled), agave syrup, or nectar, is becoming more widely known and available. If your supermarket does not stock this, it's likely that a health food store will.

Alcohol
Use *Barnivore.com*, a free online information site, to check if alcoholic beverages are vegan or vegan-friendly. Where alcohol has been used in a recipe without a substitution given, use the same amount of vegetable stock (for savory recipes), apple juice (for sweet recipes), or water in its place.

Amaranth
A small South American grain, similar in shape to quinoa though much smaller in size. When cooked, it becomes quite gelatinous and sticky. Once cooked, it's perfect as porridge or for use as a binding agent in recipes. Find with packaged grains or in bulk bins.

Arrowroot powder and tapioca starch
These thickeners are made from tropical starchy roots, and both work in a similar way to cornstarch, which can be used as a replacement.

Black salt
It's actually pink, not black. Available online and in Indian spice stores and also known as *Kala Namak*, it is pungently sulfurous, so it adds an egg-like aroma to recipes.

Brown rice syrup
Derived from brown rice, this thick liquid is less intensely sweet than agave or sugar and has a nice, almost nutty, flavor.

Buckwheat
A gluten-free grain, buckwheat has no relation to wheat, but is a "pseudo-grain" botanically related to rhubarb. Often found alongside packaged grains or in bulk bins at the market, buckwheat kernels are available toasted (known as kasha), or untoasted.

Chia seeds
These nutritional powerhouses, often called a superfood, are available whole or ground. I use the ground version (grind whole seeds in a spice grinder), as an egg replacer. (You can use flaxseeds instead; for every tsp of ground chia seeds called for in a recipe, use a tbsp of ground flaxseeds.)

Chipotle in adobo
Chipotles are dried, smoked jalapeño peppers, and adobo is a tomato-based sauce/marinade in which the chipotles are soaked. Sold in small cans, they're a little spicy and full of smoky flavor.

Chipotle or ancho chili powder
The ancho chili powder is milder and sweeter than the chipotle, but these are essentially interchangeable. If you don't have access to either, use ground chili powder.

Gluten-free flours

I use rice, millet, chickpea, quinoa, and teff flour in this book. They are all gluten-free raw grains ground to a flour. (If you can't find flour, you can grind the grains in a powerful spice grinder or blender.) Millet and quinoa flours are interchangeable. Chickpea flour tastes horrible before it's cooked or baked, so please refrain from tasting any batter containing chickpea flour!

Hemp seeds

From a strain of the hemp plant that is THC-free and perfectly safe for human consumption, hemp is another nutritional powerhouse seed with a sweet nutty taste. The addition of these seeds is optional in the recipes.

Hominy

Hominy is made from dried maize kernels treated with an alkali. Canned hominy is available wherever Central American or Latin food products are sold, if not in the supermarket. I have found no difference between the yellow and the white, so use what you can find and/or prefer.

Jackfruit, canned

A large fruit grown in the tropics, jackfruit is available canned, as young (unripe) fruit in brine (which I use) or mature (ripe) fruit in syrup. It's often available in Asian markets,

Indian spice stores, or where Latin food products are sold.

Mango chutney

Often found in supermarkets alongside the Indian cooking sauces, mango chutney is at once sweet, sour, and a little spicy on the palate. Also sold at Indian spice stores.

Marmite

Marmite is a brand-name food spread made from yeast extract, found in many supermarkets or specialty stores and online. Although a bit expensive, a little does go a long way, and it lasts indefinitely if stored in the refrigerator. An alternative is to replace each tsp of Marmite called for with 1 tsp soy sauce and ⅛ tsp liquid smoke.

Masa harina

This Mexican staple, a corn-based flour made from hominy (see left), is becoming more commonly available, especially the Maseca brand, and is always stocked in Central American or Latin markets.

Miso paste

A Japanese condiment made from fermented soy beans, miso adds a salty savoryness to dishes. The darker the miso, the stronger the flavor.

Nori

Made from seaweed, it's used to make sushi. Sometimes available in supermarkets; if not, Asian markets stock this.

Nutritional yeast

Used to add a certain savory "chees-y"ness to vegan dishes. Often found in health food stores, but some progressive supermarkets may stock this too.

Pastry (phyllo and puff)

Phyllo (also spelled Filo and Fillo) is paper-thin pastry sheets, and while commonly sold in supermarkets, you will need to check ingredients for animal ingredients and additives. Vegan puff pastry is usually found in the freezer case, alongside ready-made pie crusts.

Pomegranate molasses and tamarind paste

Sold in health food stores and Middle Eastern or Indian spice stores, both of these products are thick and sweet and sour. As you only need a little, a bottle will last a long time. If you can't find pomegranate molasses, you can easily make your own by cooking 4 cups (1 L) pomegranate juice, ½ cup (125 mL) sugar, and 1 tbsp lemon juice until thick, syrupy, and reduced to 1 cup (250 mL).

Rosewater and rose extract

Available from Middle Eastern grocers and Indian spice stores, rosewater adds a wonderful floral note anywhere it is used. Pure rose extract (which may be found with other baking extracts on your supermarket's shelves) should be used sparingly because of its intense flavor.

Soba and rice noodles

Both of these noodles are readily available from Asian markets if you can't find them in a conventional supermarket. Soba noodles are made from buckwheat flour, which is gluten-free, but may sometimes have wheat flour added, so check labels if this is an issue for you. Rice noodles are made from rice flour. Both cook quickly in water.

Spelt flour

Spelt flour is made from the whole spelt grain and has a light, almost nutty flavor. Spelt is a relative of wheat and contains gluten. If you can't find spelt flour, use whole wheat pastry flour.

Spring roll wrappers

Vegan spring roll wrappers do exist! I find them at my local Asian supermarket in the freezer section, so try looking there first. An alternative would be to use phyllo pastry cut to size and layered.

Tahini

Think peanut butter, but made from sesame seeds. You'll find this alongside the peanut (and other nut) butters. The oil often separates from the butter, so stir well before using.

Thai sweet chili sauce

A sweet chili sauce used in Thai cuisine, mainly as a dipping sauce or marinade, but I like to add it to all sorts of things. Found in most supermarkets.

Vital wheat gluten powder

Used to make seitan and provide structure to other home-made faux-meats, this is pure gluten removed from wheat flour. Often available at the supermarket in the baking aisle alongside the flour or in bulk bins. (See Three Vegan Proteins below.)

White balsamic vinegar

Milder and sweeter than the more common dark balsamic vinegar, white balsamic is available in most stores. If you don't have access to it, use apple cider vinegar.

Three Vegan Proteins, or, Beyond Tofu!

These delicious and hearty options for your dinner table are all used in the recipes in this book. I don't consider them to be "fake meat"; all are unique ingredients with their own history, flavor, and texture.

Seitan

This chewy protein is made from gluten, the protein in wheat, and is a versatile ingredient lending itself to many flavoring options and cooking styles. It is simple to make at home using vital wheat gluten (check online for recipes) and is also available pre-made. Seitan and vital wheat gluten are both available at most supermarkets, health food stores, and online.

Tempeh

This fermented, whole soybean-based protein is a traditional food from Indonesia. It is widely available in supermarkets and health food stores, both in pure soybean and combination ingredient forms. It readily absorbs marinades and lends itself to many cooking styles.

TVP

Textured Vegetable Protein is also a soy-based food, though made from soy flour rather than the whole bean, and as such it is more processed than either tempeh or tofu. It is quick-cooking and absorbs liquid and flavor as it cooks, making it easy to adapt to a variety of cuisines.

Theme Menus for Picnics & Barbecues

To help inspire you for your next great outdoor gathering, here are some recipe suggestions to prepare for special occasions or for special "theme nights" (or days). Choose as many recipes from the following lists as you like, and add more as desired! Each recipe generally serves 4–6 as part of a spread, so each menu will be suitable for numbers up to 10.

You'll find some of the recipes are listed under more than one heading—on purpose! The recipes lend themselves to varied themes, so use these suggestions as a starting point to create your own.

These menus make it easy when you want to make it potluck—everyone attending the picnic or barbecue just needs to bring one of the dishes on the list and their beverage of choice. Easy!

Best of British
Brandied Tempeh Pâté (p. 69)
Cider-Battered Tofu (p. 49)
Coronation Tofu (p. 91)
Mini-Quiche (p. 38)
Nutty Cauliflower Salad (p. 126)
Groovy Multi-Grain Burgers (p. 154)
Corn Relish (p. 80)
Strawberry & Basil Scones (p. 198)
Berry Swirl Cheesecake (p. 216)
Lavender Cookies (p. 229)

Down Under
Cider-Battered Tofu (p. 49)
Beet & Bean Burgers (p. 153)
Pan Pacific Tofu (p. 161)
Jalapeño & Cherry Jam (p. 82)
Banana Cookies (p. 233)

Japanese Fusion
Caper & Edamame Dip (p. 61)
South American Sushi (p. 34)
Garlicky Miso Dressing (p. 121)
Smoky Soba Noodle Salad (p. 137)
Lime & Ginger Tahini Tofu Skewers
(p. 165)
Coconut Ice Cream (p. 210)
Cherry & Almond Cookies (p. 227)

Latin Flavors
South American Sushi (p. 34)
Quinoa & Avocado 'Slaw (p. 131)
Chipotle & Cilantro Lentil Burger
(p. 152)
Mojito-Inspired Tofu (p. 162)
Massaged Red Onions & Cumin
(p. 84)
Melon & Corn Salsa (p. 75)

Muffins of the Americas (p. 190)
Quinoa & Pineapple Muffins (p. 197)
Coconut Ice Cream (p. 210)
Spicy Spelt Chocolate Chip Cookies
(p. 224)

Mediterranean Cruising
Chilled Arugula & Artichoke Dip
(p. 62)
Grilled Eggplant Sandwiches
(p. 101)
Poached Garlic & White Wine
Dressing (p. 116)
Raspberry Balsamic Dressing
(p. 115)
Garlic Sage Sausages (p. 160)
Grilled Zucchini Sticks (p. 176)
Raspberry Balsamic Glazed Seitan
(p. 171)
Artichoke & Sunflower Seed Pesto
(p. 79)
Basil & Blueberry Cookies (p. 228)
Espresso Cookies (p. 231)

Nutty about Nuts
White Bean & Peanut Dip (p. 63)
Walnut & Mushroom Pâté (p. 70)
Nut & Seed Crackers (p. 183)
Spicy Caramelized Pecans (p. 31)
Smoky & Salty Roasted Nuts (p. 30)
Nutonnaise (p. 111)
Peanut Potato Salad (p. 134)
Hazelnut Latte Cupcakes (p. 212)
Chocolate Peanut Chunk Cookies
(p. 223)
Gluten-free Nut & Seed Cookies
(p. 235)

Allergen Lists

The following recipes are grouped by the major allergens they contain. Please always double check labels of ingredients you purchase.

Contains Gluten

Bites, Nibbles & Finger Foods
Cider-Battered Tofu (p. 49)
Mini-Quiche (crust only, optional) (p. 38)
Mini-Spring Rolls with Chili Lime Dipping Sauce (pastry only) (p. 45)
Samosa Spring Rolls (pastry only) (p. 47)
Zesty Broccoli Parcels (pastry only) (p. 35)

Sandwiches & Spreads
Aussie Falafel (bread only) (p. 102)
Grilled Eggplant Sandwiches (bread only) (p. 101)
Meat-y Ball Sandwich (p. 106)
Pita Po' Boys (p. 104)
Twice-Fried Seitan Bites (p. 36)

Ready-Built Salads
Creamy Macaroni Salad (pasta only) (p. 140)
Hearty Three-Grain Salad (p. 147)
Israeli Couscous Tabouleh (p. 139)
Smoky Soba Noodle Salad (possibly noodles) (p. 137)
Southwestern Spelt Salad (p. 143)

On the Grill
Beet & Bean Burgers (p. 153)
Garlic & Sage Sausages (p. 160)
Mango Chutney Seitan Strips (p. 172)
Raspberry Balsamic-Glazed Seitan (p. 171)
Seitan Burgers (p. 157)
Seitan Satay with Spicy Peanut Sauce (p. 173)
Seitan Skewers with Peach Salsa (p. 170)

Baking & Brunch
Baklava Scones (p. 199)
Banana Spelt Waffles (p. 196)
Buckwheat & Onion Mini-Loaves (p. 189)
Corn & Olive Focaccia (p. 187)
Garlic Breadsticks (p. 185)
Loaded Banana Bread (p. 201)
Muffins of the Americas (p. 190)
Nut & Seed Crackers (p. 183)
Plain Rolls or Loaves (p. 186)
Quinoa & Pineapple Muffins (p. 197)
Savory Sausage Muffins (p. 191)
Strawberry & Basil Scones (p. 198)
Triple Chocolate Waffles (p. 195)

Desserts
Apricot Bundt Cake (p. 214)
Banana & Carrot Cake (p. 211)
Berry Swirl Cheesecake (p. 216)
Chilled Blueberry Chocolate Pie (pastry only) (p. 219)
Hazelnut Latte Cupcakes (p. 212)
Maple & Walnut Cheesecake (p. 218)

Cookies
Banana Cookies (p. 233)
Basil & Berry Cookies (p. 228)
Chai Tea Cookies (p. 230)
Cherry & Almond Cookies (p. 227)
Chocolate Peanut Chunk Cookies (p. 223)
Espresso Cookies (p. 231)
Lavender Cookies (p. 229)
Masa Chocolate Chip Cookies (p. 225)
No Bake Oatmeal Cookies (p. 236)
Spicy Spelt Chocolate Chip Cookies (p. 224)
Sugar-free Sugar Cookies (p. 234)

Contains Nuts

Basic Recipes
Dry Chees-y Mix (p. 18)

Bites, Nibbles & Finger Foods
Mini-Quiche (p. 38)
Tomato & Olive Tarts (p. 40)
Smoky & Salty Roasted Nuts (p. 30)
Spicy Caramelized Pecans (p. 31)
Walnut & Mushroom Pâté (p. 70)
White Bean & Peanut Dip (p. 63)

Dips, Sauces, Condiments & Accompaniments
Chilled Arugula & Artichoke Dip (p. 62)

Contains Soy

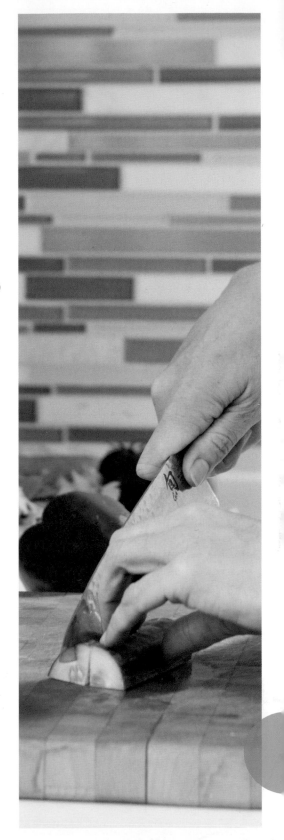

Acknowledgments

Once again, an incredible team of testers assisted me in getting these recipes ready to be presented in book form. A round of applause (let's make it a standing ovation!) for:

Stefanie Amann, Oregon
Courtney Blair, Minnesota
Kelly Cavalier, Ontario, Canada
Megan Clarke, Alberta, Canada
Jamie Coble, Washington
Melissa Cormier, Pennsylvania
Linda Findon, Rotorua, New Zealand
Debyi Kucera, Arizona
Kim Lahn, Arizona
Kate Lawson, Massachusetts
Lee Ann Light, Colorado
Tania Osborn, North Carolina
Celia Ozereko, Virginia
Theresa Pettray, Townsville,
    Australia
Shirley Saliniemi, Finland
Michélle Saunders, Wellington,
    New Zealand
Amy Silver, Auckland, New Zealand
Penny Tayler, Melbourne, Australia
Fiona Wellgreen, Wellington,
    New Zealand
Liz Wyman, England

I also need to mention the following folks:

Thanks to Brian Lam at Arsenal Pulp Press for picking up this idea and turning it into a book. To Susan, Gerilee, and the rest of the APP team—awesome to work with you, hope to do so again real soon!

Tracey Kusiewicz from Foodie Photography—you are (seriously) magical!

To the authors who provided inspiration without knowing it, and are wonderful in their own right—Isa Chandra Moskowitz and Terry Hope Romero, cheers!

Love to my Mum and Dad for all the assistance they always provide.

Love also to my siblings: Sonia, Fiona, Linda, and Iain. Without my being the eldest of all you lot, I'd never have learned to cook and bake as early as I did. Love, too, to my first-ever niece, Bethany Loren.

And, as always, my wonderful husband and daughters who really are my inspiration and my reason for doing all I do.

Index

CARLA KELLY, a vegan for almost ten years, has worked at hotels around the world. She is the author of two previous cookbooks, *Quick and Easy Bake Sale* and *Quick and Easy Vegan Slow Cooking* and operates the food website The Year of the Vegan (*veganyear.blogspot.ca*). She lives in Burnaby, BC, Canada.

Find her on Facebook at Carla.Kelly.Vegan